Quick Guide to
the Wines of
All the Americas

Quick Guide to the Wines of All the Americas

ROBERT JAY MISCH

Drawings by Charles McVicker

DOUBLEDAY & COMPANY, INC.

Garden City, New York

1977

DEDICATION

Many wines improve with age. So why not inscriptions? I shall simply annotate what I have used as a preface for five books heretofore; viz.

To my consultant, confidante, aide-de-camp, director, arbiter, companion and partner—Janet, my wife.

JXXXXB

APPRECIATION

A heartfelt thank you to the Wine Institute of California (especially Harvey Posert and Tony Kahmann) and to my many dear wine friends of California and New York, who are the kindest and most dedicated lot I have ever had the pleasure of knowing, and to other wine men from Tierra del Fuego to Baffin Land, who have helped me in this endeavor.

R.J.M.

Library of Congress Cataloging in Publication Data

Misch, Robert Jay.
  Quick guide to the wines of all the Americas.

  Includes index.
  1. Wine and wine making—United States.   2. Wine and wine making—America.   I. Title.
TP557.M57   641.2′2′0973
ISBN 0-385-06469-1
Library of Congress Catalog Card Number 76–23783

CONTENTS

PREFACE

When faced with a blank—oh! so blank—piece of paper and a pencil at the ready (yes, I am one of those who has never mastered the art of thinking while punching a typewriter), many thoughts course through my head. You should know some of them the better to understand this book—what it is meant to be, what it isn't meant to be, why it may have shortcomings in some respects and why it may succeed in others.

This is the fifth Quick Guide that I have essayed for Doubleday & Company. (The others are *Quick Guide to Wine, Quick Guide to Spirits, Quick Guide to the World's Most Famous Recipes, Quick Guide to Cheese.*)

When a QUICK GUIDE TO THE WINES OF ALL THE AMERICAS was proposed I took a somewhat dim view of the enterprise, not because I was opposed to such content but because I felt there were ever so many books on the subject by many distinguished authors (a number of them quite recent), and that another seemed de trop. But then it was cogently pointed out to me that the same might have been said about any or all of my other titles at the time of their inception. André Simon had produced dozens of books on the wines of the world; Frank Schoonmaker and Alexis Lichine had written classics on phases of the subject; Cyril Ray had contributed from abroad, as had Hallgarten, Waugh, Rainbird, and others. In cheese, Androuet had seemed to have produced the definitive volume; Daiches had written with finality on scotch whisky—and so on. But they (Doubleday, that is, in the persons of my editors Ferris Mack, Clara Claasen, and Louise Gault) pointed out that in most cases these were lengthy and exhaustive tomes and that, in general, the casual wine drinker, or wine drinker novice, didn't really want "to know all that." Rather, he was interested in knowing just enough to enjoy what he was doing a little bit more, enough not to be intimidated by a sommelier or headwaiter, enough to hold his own in the milieu of his peers, enough not to be "taken" by tradesmen or patronized by "wine snobs." This, they told me, is what my other slim volumes had accomplished—and, they added, with ill-concealed flattery, "successfully"—and hence this is the reason for the book you now hold.

If you are an average American, your wine complement is at least three quarters Californian, 10% from other states, primarily New York, and 15% imported. Only a modicum of the imported is from this Western Hemisphere; the rest is from the traditional wine countries of Europe.

In accordance with the tenets laid down by my previous Guides, I shall endeavor to serve up a lot of information in a laconic and, I hope, light but not frivolous manner. I know at the start I shall leave out some facts, even some new vineyards, that should have been included; I know I shall err in certain aspects of reportage; I know that the time lag between writing and publication is a considerable problem; but I also know that forgiveness should be in your hearts because there is hardly a subject that is changing so rapidly, constantly, and confusingly.

Now that I have tried to protect my flanks, on to the attack in QUICK GUIDE TO THE WINES OF ALL THE AMERICAS.

The Hemisphere

When people speak of American wine, most of them chauvinistically mean the wines of the United States and particularly those of California. Matter of fact, they speak of themselves as the only Americans, forgetting that Brazilians and Mexicans and Canadians are also residents of the Americas, and as "American" as they are.

From a vinicultural point of view, the best wine grapes are a Temperate Zone crop. The great wine grapes—sometimes referred to as the "noble grapes"—the grapes that make Bordeaux, Burgundies, Rhines and Moselles, Cabernets Sauvignons, Pinots Noirs, Chardonnays, etc.—all grow best where the climate is temperate, where the days may be warm but where the mists or fogs or soil conditions give the vines' roots relief some part of the day—else the grapes get a *brûleé* or burnt taste. These top grapes are almost all members of the vinifera family, the grapes of the heartland of Europe stretching from Oporto in Portugal, through France from Rheims on the north to Lyons on the south, through Germany and Switzerland from Coblenz to Geneva, through Austria, Czechoslovakia, and Hungary from Prague to Budapest. Below this belt is another climatic strip, the Mediterranean, which includes most of Portugal and Spain, Provence and the Rhône Valley in France, most all of Italy, Yugoslavia, Greece, and Turkey.

California, which is planted to Europe's vinifera grapes, displays similar climatic variations between the cool-climate grapes —of Napa, Sonoma and parts of Livermore, Santa Clara, and the Salinas River Valley of the north coast around Monterey—

and the Mediterranean-climate grapes of the great Central Valley, San Joaquin, and on down to the Cucamonga area outside of Los Angeles.

There can be no doubt about it, the Temperate Zone grapes are superior for wine. While it is self-evident that Piedmont in Italy and the Rhône Valley can produce outstanding wines, while some of the Mediterranean-type grapes can create some excellent wines, it is the "cooler" grapes that give us the majority of the world's great wines, in Europe as well as here.

Two other factors might be mentioned at this point:

1. The advent of the so-called "hybrid" grape, a new grape family linking the hot- and cold-climate grapes. The world-famous School of Enology, or Wine Technology, of the University of California at Davis, California, and the one at Geneva Station in New York, as well as others abroad, have devoted years and prodigious effort to creating new grape species by grafts that share good wine-making propensities together with resistance to hot and cold weather and to the phylloxera (a plant louse devastator). Thanks to their efforts, and additional help from abroad, such grapes as the Emerald Riesling, the Ruby Cabernet, Carnelian, Chelois, Seibels, etc., have been developed and are producing some interesting wines.

2. The recognition that climate, and more recently mini-climate, is the single most important criterion of the fitness of a location for grape growing, certainly more than soil.

CALIFORNIA

As far back as 1938, California was divided into five "regions" based on their average daily temperatures during the grape-growing season. This was done by keeping accurate tabs on "degree days"; e.g., the number of degrees the mean temperature exceeded 50° F. If the day averaged 80°, then it was expressed as a 30 degree day and added as such to the total. Region I embraces the coolest parts of Napa and Sonoma (2500 degree days or less). Region II (2500 to 3000 degree days) takes in all the rest of Napa and Sonoma—even some of Santa Clara to Monterey. Region III (with 3000 to 3500 degree days) includes Livermore, parts of Santa Clara, and Salinas Valley (Monterey). Region IV (3500 to 4000 degree days) includes Lodi, Davis, and the northern San Joaquin Valley. Region V (over 4000 degree days) is the Sacramento Valley and the southern San Joaquin.

At one time such broad, sweeping measurements were considered adequate. Not so now—the small climatic differences even within a single vineyard are being studied for their important bearing on the types of grapes best suited for planting and hence for optimum quality of the wines produced.

NEW YORK AND THE EAST

When we take a hop, skip, and jump across the continent to the second most important vineyard area—New York (and neighboring Pennsylvania and Ohio)—while it is still the Temperate Zone, as the saying goes, some Temperate Zones are more temperate than others. New York's winters can be brutally frigid.

The vinifera grapes of Europe and California are not suited to the climate (with some vitally important exceptions). Hence, most of the vines and grapes used are what are known as the labrusca variety—descendants of the wild grapes Leif the Lucky is said to have discovered when he sailed along the coast of what is now Canada and spotted Newfoundland covered with wild vines. He called it Vineland.

The characteristics of labrusca are twofold: extreme hardiness and a wild, grapey, puckery sort of taste that is transmitted to the wine made from them. The enologist calls the taste "foxy." You'll call it grapey. That doesn't mean it's necessarily inferior to the vinifera-made wine; it's simply different.

However, in recent years vinifera species have been successfully grown in New York, with the inordinate skill of Konstantin Frank and his steadfast supporter, the now retired Charles Fournier of Gold Seal, leading the way. Include Mark Miller of Benmarl Wineries in that company.

It takes patience in selecting and propagating the hardier clones*; it takes skill in selecting the proper locations—usually hard by large bodies of water, which act as moderators of temperature changes; it takes a bit of luck and a whispered prayer that no "old-fashioned" terror of a winter comes along. But it has worked, and some of the results are spectacular.

Another interesting development of late is the acquisition of West Coast vineyards by East Coast vintners. A few of these wines are being bottled for what they are, but the largest percentage is being used to blend with Eastern wines to counterbalance the high acidity and smooth out the labrusca.

Then, too, the experimental Geneva Station, the Eastern counterpart of the Davis Enology School in California, and the great hybridizers—Seibel, Seyve-Villard, etc.—have contributed greatly by producing the reverse of Davis' "hot" grapes, hybridiz-

* A "clone" to the botanist is a plant "sport" or scion different in some respect from the parent and the other progeny.

4

ing French varieties on hardy American root stock, to give us hardy and better wine grapes such as Chelois, Baco Noir, Aurora —new grapes from which to make new Eastern wines. Delawares, Catawbas, Niagaras, Scuppernongs, Concords—look to your laurels. A new era is at hand in Eastern wine production.

THE OTHER AMERICAS

Outside of the United States the Temperate Zone is of course off and running, and producing grapes and wines well worth discussion and experimentation.

Canada   There are two main vineyard areas in Canada, both hugging the borders of the United States and both next to large bodies of water for the moderation of what can be severely cold winters.

The first, the Eastern district, is that finger of Ontario that pokes down between Lakes Ontario and Erie, past Canadian Niagara Falls within sight of Buffalo across the lake. Here the labrusca grape flourishes although, of late, the same sequence of events has taken place as in the Eastern United States; viz., the planting of certain viniferas and the introduction of hardy French hybrids. Matter of fact, it is claimed by Bright & Co., near Niagara Falls, that they were the first in the East to grow vinifera, before Konstantin Frank had ever left Germany.

The other Canadian grape area is in British Columbia, huddled around Lake Okanagan and running south to the Washington State line. The wines made here are akin to those of California, just as the Eastern Canadians are kissin' cousins of New York. A little farther north from either group of vineyards, and you'd be out of the Temperate Zone and trying to raise grapes in the tundra!

Mexico Mexico, too, has its temperature problems. The southern part of the country, certainly from Mexico City south, becomes more and more tropical as it approaches the countries of Central America—land more suited to bananas than grapes. While no part of Mexico is truly temperate, as we mean it, the central plateau, a mile or more high, helps make up in height for what it lacks in longitude. Some of the best grapes are grown in extreme northerly Baja California. But the most celebrated grape-growing area is the valley around the provincial city of Parras, said to be the oldest vine-growing area on the continent, dating back to 1593.

Chile Chile is the most blessed of the South American republics —in wine, that is. It is so long and thin in shape that a good piece is indeed in the Temperate Zone and hence can raise the noble vinifera grapes and make extremely successful wines from them. The best wine areas are south of Santiago in the Maipo Valley. There such old standbys as Cabernets Sauvignons and Francs, Merlot and Malbec, Pinots Noirs and Blancs thrive, owing to equable temperatures, the lean soil, and the incidence of rainfall, thanks to the wall provided by the stupendous Andes.

Brazil Most of the winegrowing in this generally tropical country is confined to Rio Grande do Sul down near the basin of the La Plata, bordering Uruguay and Argentina. Not too much reaches us—nor need we fret too much about that.

Argentina This is another matter. Argentina is so situated that it touches tropical Brazil's jungles, borders the Antarctic's ice floes, and sandwiches in the middle a nice slice of temperate clime. The industry is primarily in the far west, in the provinces of Mendoza, San Juan, and Rio Negro. The Argentines produce a staggering three quarters of a billion gallons, and drink an equally staggering 22 gallons per person per annum. The wineries are amazingly modern and some of the vinifera wines are remarkably good. Most of the production, however, is for local consumption—from the Criollas (the old Mission grapes). The major problem is water, partially solved by diverting the melting Andean snows to irrigation ditches. Such irrigation doesn't improve the wine, but without it there would be none.

That is the temperature picture of grape husbandry in the Western Hemisphere. I may have missed a few plantings in Uruguay, for which I may be forgiven, and neglected to mention plantings in states other than California and New York—but rest assured, this is not an oversight. They will be referred to in a later passage.

What Is Wine?
Today and Tomorrow

Wine is simply the fermented juice of the grape (wine can be made from other fruit, and much is—commercially and at home —but for the purposes of this slim volume I shall stay with grape wine, commercially produced). Fermentation means the phenomenon whereby yeast, specially injected or naturally growing on the skin of the grape, attacks the sugar in the juice and converts it to alcohol, giving off clouds of CO_2 (carbon dioxide) in the process. Fourteen per cent alcohol is normally the upper limit. At that point the yeast is killed by the strong spirit. It literally commits suicide. If unfermented sugar is left, when the 14% is reached, then you have a sweet wine. If none or very little is left, the wine is said to be dry.

If you add nothing else, do nothing else, you have "table" wine; if you add grape brandy, you have "fortified" wine; flavor it with barks, herbs, berries, etc., and you have "flavored" wine; capture some CO_2 in the bottle during a record fermentation and you have "sparkling" wine. And that's all the wines there are.

IS THERE A WINE BOOM?

Well, yes and no. If you compare the United States' consumption of, and interest in, wine today with that of even ten years ago, the answer is a resounding "yes."

If you compare it with the intake of our Latin American and European friends, we have a very long way to go. We consume just about 1½ gallons of wine per year per adult. The statistics (and don't take these as gospel but they'll give you the idea): Italy—29 gallons; Spain—28 gallons; France—26 gallons; Argentina—22 gallons; give or take a gallon.

However, if you compare these figures we are on our way:

	1960 (millions of gallons)	1974–75 (millions of gallons)
By Type		
Table wines	53 (32%)	214 (59%)
Dessert wines	87 (54%)	67 (18%)
Other wines	23 (14%)	87 (23%) (includes popular fruit wines, sparkling and flavored)
By Origin		
California	129 (67%)	272 (73.6%)
Other states	24 (22%)	48 (13.0%)
Imports	11 (11%)	49 (13.4%)

Don't take these figures too literally. It is the trend that's important—the trend shows table wines growing from a third of all wine consumed to well over half—at the expense of the fortified or "sweet" wines (the Sherries, Ports, Muscatels), which

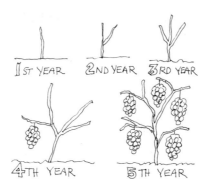

1ST YEAR   2ND YEAR   3RD YEAR

4TH YEAR   5TH YEAR

dropped from 54% of all fifteen years ago to a bare 18% today. This usually indicates an increase in a nation's sophistication in drinking.

Over the past year the growth rate has slackened some. It had to. Growing at a rate of 10% or more a year is just not in the cards. Growth is never in a straight line; with every little zig there must be a zag. The amazing thing is that we've zigged as much as we have, compared to our more traditional beverages: beer (20 gallons per person) and hard liquor (2 gallons per person).

It must be borne in mind that grape husbandry is a mighty ticklish business. You can't just turn a spigot off and on. It takes a lot of work just to prepare ground for the vine. Then a vineyard must be carefully planted to allow for mechanical cropping, irrigation (if any), fertilization, and spraying. Then the best vine stock must be secured and planted by experts. And then sit back four years before you even see a grape—and five before you're harvesting for real. That's why, with the growth boom of the seventies, by 1974 California's fine grape acreage had nearly doubled, record harvests followed, and—grape prices fell about half.

It's going to be a battle for survival, with producers caught between spiraling costs of labor and materials and consumer resistance to price increases.

Just when you'll be reading this of course I can't know. But I will go out on this limb. As this is written in 1975–76, problems loom large for the wine industry of this country (and the importer as well). I'm only the second son of a third son, and not the seventh son of a prophet, but I am optimistic on wine. The United States has learned to like wine . . . is learning to like it more and more. It was the young people who led the way. They will be the prime age group for consumption for years, and they'll carry their liking with them on into maturity.

A PROGNOSTICATION FROM THE BANK OF AMERICA

By 1980 the B. of A. predicts annual wine sales of 650 million gallons (today 400 million gallons). Of this, California will do over

400 million (today 235 million) but California's 70% of the total today will fall to 63%. Imports will rise to 20% from 14.6% and "other states" will do 17% compared to today's 15½%. Table wines (less than 14% alcohol) will represent 72% of 1980's sales (it was 30% in 1960). An increase in the number of adults in the United States (as people live longer) is one contributing factor, they point out. Right on, B. of A.

WHO IS THE WINE BUYER?

67% are married and 22% single, compared with 70% and 16% among the general public.

43% are under thirty-five compared with 30% of all Americans.

53% live in the suburbs and 32% in the city.

36% are living in the Northeast compared to 25% of the population; 28% live in the West compared with 17% of all Americans.

47% attended college compared with 25% of the nation.

44% enjoy a family income of $15,000 a year or more compared with 26% of all Americans.

55% of all wine is bought by women (some say 70%, but add, "often they buy what they're told by their husbands")—48% buy only American, 24% only imported, and 28% have "no preference." 35% of all wine is bought at the supermarket.

WHAT IS STILL NEEDED?

What will be necessary to spur the wine vogue? Lots of things as I see it:

1. Greater knowledge of wines on the part of the consumer, by tasting and trying—and yes, reading a little on the subject and listening a little too.

2. A more sensible pricing attitude on the part of the restaurateur. It is in the restaurant that the first acquaintance with wine often takes place. Pricing wines exorbitantly is as foolish as it is immoral.

3. Greater knowledge on the part of the retailer and his clerks, so that they can impart information to their customers.

4. Easier buying. When Maine took table wines out of liquor stores and put them into supermarkets, sales of table wines rose 400%. After all, women buy 55–70% of all wine. On the other hand, the wine and liquor store provides advice and counsel to the tyro buyer that is not forthcoming from a cold, inanimate pile of bottles in a bin or aisle-end.

5. Getting away from treating wine as a special occasion, celebration, out-of-the-ordinary drink rather than a normal, regular, daily supplement to the diet.

6. A settling down of prices. It is vital that the price tags of imports and United States wines settle down for a while, and at realistic levels. The industry must end the speculative gyrations of the last several years. It seems on its way to doing this.

7. The impending switch over to the metric system of bottling (mandatory January 1, 1979). This will do for the bottle what new and simplified nomenclature does for the label. Then there will be uniformity and less infighting between United States and European producers as to which is mulcting the public out of an ounce or two. It will shape up like this:

Today		Metric	
Present Terminology	Ounces	New Terminology	Ounces
Tenth	12.8	Medium	12.68
Fifth	25.6	Regular	25.36
Quart	32	Liter	33.81
Magnum	51.2	1½ liters	50.72

WHAT'S NEW IN THE
VINEYARDS?

You don't care—or do you?—how wine is made as long as it tastes good and is at a price you can afford. But these two desiderata depend on developments in the wineries and in the growing fields. I've noted many new wrinkles as I've toured the world of wine—from France to Argentina to California and New York.

Thanks to innovative procedures developed at the great enological stations of the world—in which grouping our own Davis takes a very front seat—better wines are made today than ever before. Don't believe it that Grandpa drank better. If there's a bottle from his cellar still around and still drinkable, its excellence isn't so much from the procedures used then as from the mellowing finger of time.

I'm not a wine maker or a grape grower, but I have noted such developments as:

1. Rushing grapes from picker to crusher—sometimes even crushing in the field.

2. Mechanical harvesting—not perfected yet but on its way. The "beating" picker, which literally beats the grapes off the vine with rods, is a real step forward, if some of the leaves that go along with the grapes in the process can be discarded.

3. If irrigation has to be practiced at all—and it must be in certain climates—the "drip" system by which a membrane admits water drop by drop at a regular rate, and directed right at the roots—not in a widespread arc—seems sensationally good. (Irrigation increases yield per acre by about double—8 tons average compared to 4 or less for certain varieties. Overproduction can be as bad on a grapevine as on a mother.)

4. The planting of better and better grapes, especially in California, is of the first importance. In 1974, 35,000 new wine-grape acres were planted, of which 4000 acres were Cabernet Sauvi-

gnon; Chardonnay, 2000; Pinot Noir, 1500. Wine-grape planting was 67,000 acres in 1973; 62,000 in 1972. All will come into bearing in three to four years from planting. Today's figures for wine grapes: 181,000 acres with 140,000 more still to come into bearing.

A glut? Possibly. Prices for top grape varieties have receded from unrealistic prices of up to $1000 a ton to less than half that much. But the industry has faith in steadily growing consumption, and at worst we'll all be getting better grapes in our wine, and hence better wine.

5. The vintner is learning a great deal about mini-climates—planting grape types to match physical growing conditions, planting test batches inside other plantings for comparison purposes. This can only result in the greatest desideratum of all—fewer wines from each winery, and concentration on the wines each makes best.

6. In the winery, greater attention is being paid to cool fermentation, to lighter crushing, to the use of less filtration for a gutsier product, to faster handling of white grapes and wine to minimize oxidation, and to longer aging for reds. Mention should also be made of carbonic maceration, whereby grapes are placed in the fermenter whole and the juice fermented inside the skins. For young drinkin' wines, such as the Gamay Beaujolais, the process produces interesting results.

7. And the industry itself is giving more attention to raising the percentage of a varietal required for a grape "name" wine (Cabernet Sauvignon, Pinot Chardonnay or Chardonnay, Zinfandel, etc.). The present 51% was not handed down from on high. Why not 60% or 75%? A hundred per cent is not against the law, you know.

It is also questioning the correctness of permitting a winery to claim "Estate Bottled" even if the grapes used are from non-contiguous vineyards sometimes separated by many miles. Finally, mirabile dictu, United States wine makers—as honest, capable,

skilled, and decent a lot as you're likely to meet—are demonstrating the self-confidence and security that presage a final end to the remnants of chauvinism and overconcern with the other guy and his wine, whoever and wherever he may be. After all, a grape is a pump, not a thing unto itself. It is what the soil and mini-climate make it. A Cabernet Sauvignon grown in St. Helena is not exactly the same as one from the Médoc—for these reasons. Both places produce good grapes. Both produce good wines. They needn't be the same. After all, is a French-Canadian French? Or Canadian? No, he's something of each. We should, I believe, recognize this and stop some of the "Isn't this as good as that?" tasting and tests.

8. Free-run wine vs. press wine provides another interesting argument. Free-run is the juice from the first crush. If the skins are pressed again, you have press wine. Some vintners feel a little press adds tannin and guts to the wine.

Another term you'll hear is "botrytis" and/or "pourriture noble." This is a disease very late-picked grapes can acquire. It cracks the skins, lets air and sun in, evaporates some of the water, and leaves a very rich sugar-filled pulp. When such grapes are fermented, they leave unfermented sugar in the wine which gives it the "Sauternes" luscious quality.

9. For New York and Eastern states, much of the foregoing applies, and additionally the efforts go on for more and better hybrids, larger planting of viniferas, and less dependence on water and sugar to reduce the high acidity of labrusca grapes by blending with the wines of California and/or their own vinifera and hybrid wines.

10. One of the most fascinating developments of the last several years has been the proliferation of small, specialized wineries, some making as little as a few thousand cases a year, and often the wine never leaves the state of origin. Many of those vintners produce excellent wines, often at quite high prices. However, it is just as silly to equate smallness with excellence as the opposite would be. Many of the larger wineries produce wines of quality that need take no back seat to the boutique vintner's product.

11. One of the most important recent developments in the California vineyards has been the organization of the California Association of Winegrape Growers. Until now, relatively unrepresented and powerless, the growers of wine grapes were at the mercy of the wine makers, who made the market and set the prices. Obviously one group is as important as the other, and they are mutually dependent. Now they are organized in the districts of California and can speak with a unified voice in dealing with their customers, the wineries, and in solving their many mutual problems—particularly overproduction.

A Little Background

The great and growing wine industry of the United States didn't spring full-blown from the forehead of Zeus. It sprang, or rather crept, from the fumbling beginnings of the Missions of California to the sophisticated wine-producing factories of Gallo and Almadén and Taylor. The legend of Leif the Lucky making wine in a hollow stone we shall leave where it belongs—as a pretty legend.

But the Mission Fathers were something else. They were for real. One, Fra Serra, brought cuttings from Mexican vines and planted them along the Camino Real as the Missions proliferated northward. They made mighty poor wine—and still do. Alas, someone is always blasting the memory of the good old days! Incidentally, the Missions, rather than being simply religious centers, were, I am told, a knee-jerk response to the construction of a series of Russian-built fortifications stretching from Russian Alaska down through western Canada. The more things change, the more they are the same!

The real beginning of the California miracle is generally attributed to a Hungarian gentleman named Agoston Harászthy. His chroniclers delight to make him a count. Count or no account, he made good wine at Buena Vista, his home pad. As he put it, the California soil and climate could produce "as noble a

wine as any country on the face of the globe." So impressive was he to those who would listen that the state of California in 1861 sent him to Europe to corral cuttings of the best European stocks for transplantation. Being a man who couldn't take a joke, he proceeded to liberate 100,000 or more cuttings—some say 300,000! But his timing was poor. The American Civil War had begun. People were more interested in Shiloh than in Sirah, in Sumter than in Sauvignon. The poor Count was left to plant the shoots with only the help of his sons. The state, to its egregious discredit, even refused to pay him. If you must know the end of this unhappy saga, he left for Central America. In Nicaragua, so 'tis said, he inadvertently fell into a stream one day and became a Hungarian goulash for an alligator.

His work lived after him. The beginnings of the vinifera plantings of all the noble grapes, and some not so noble, can be traced to these original cuttings. It was helter-skelter planting at that, for not too much was known about planting certain varieties in cooler climes. Planting even great grapes in hot areas still results in mediocre wines. And besides, the native sons didn't see much difference between table grapes and wine grapes, between warm-country vines and cool. Result—a plethora of mediocre wines named after European climes—bearing little or no resemblance to their namesakes. California Burgundy, California Sauternes—these were the order of the day. It has taken a number of decades for California to learn the elements of viticulture—to discover the world of the fine varietals—to plant wine grapes for wine and table grapes for raisins.

By the same token, it has taken New York and other Eastern states a long time to learn how to treat with the *Vitis labrusca* varieties in wine making—to realize that new ways in viniculture can produce better wines from these grapey, "foxy" grapes, that hybridizing is one solution to tyrannical Eastern winters, and that wise selection, of stock and location, can make the husbandry of the vinifera in the frigid East a viable thing.

THE KINDS OF WINE

For the novice in wine, it is frightening just to behold the forest of bottles on the shelves of an average wine and spirits shop, or to contemplate the many pages of gobbledygook of a reasonably adequate wine list.

Be of stout heart. Just as clutch, gears, brake, accelerator, etc., finally sort themselves out when you learn to drive, so a little learning (*not* a "dangerous thing" in wine) will soon separate all those bottles for you into four major divisions:

1. **Table Wines**—wines which, by definition, are drunk "at table" with food. They are natural wines, or should be—simply the juice of the grape, fermented, then fined and filtered, aged according to the wine type and the vintner's decision. The alcoholic content is what the sugar in the grape juice produces naturally when attacked by the yeast—usually from about 9% to 13%.

2. **Fortified Wines**—wines which have had their alcoholic content raised, by the addition of grape brandy, to 18% to 22%. The prime examples are Sherry, Porto, Madeira. Such wines are usually consumed as apéritif wines—before the meal; as dessert wines—after the meal; or as between-meals wines.

3. **Flavored Wines**—wines that have been artificially flavored with barks and berries, herbs and spices. Vermouth is by far the best known, but many proprietary brands of apéritifs, closely guarded as to formula, come in this category: Dubonnet, St. Raphaël, Byrrh, etc.

4. **Sparkling Wines**—wines which have had an induced secondary fermentation, and the CO_2 gas produced captured in the bottle, resulting in the familiar bubbles of Champagne, Asti Spumante, Sekt, Sparkling Anjou, etc. It might be appropriate here to mention that there are several kinds of sparkling wines:
1) "Méthode Champenoise" or Champagne method, as used in France, means a wine made to ferment a second time in the bot-

tle, the CO_2 gas bubbles captured, the impurities of fermentation removed by intricate processes—the wine never leaving the bottle of its birth. The label reads "Fermented in *this* bottle." 2) "Transfer." Second fermentation is in the bottle, but to remove impurities bottles are emptied into a tank, the wine clarified and rebottled in other bottles. The label reads, "Fermented in *the* bottle." 3) Bulk or "Charmat": second fermentation is done entirely in the tank, wine then bottled. 4) CO_2 injected, just like Coke. 'Nuff said.

So much for *all* wines. There is another categorization of wines based on content and usually associated with California—though the East is now using the nomenclature and so even are some European producers. I refer to the breakdown of wines as varietal, generic, and proprietary.

A. The "Varietals." These wines are the princes of the blood. They are the best, by and large, that California (as well as New York and other Eastern states and some other American countries) can produce. The word is derived from "variety"—the variety of the grape(s) from which the wine is primarily produced. United States laws permit a wine to be called after the grape if the mix contains a minimum of 51% of that grape and derives its predominant taste, aroma, and characteristics from that variety. Of late, a movement has begun to revise the requirement upward. The proponents of the change point out that a minority of 49% of anything a vintner chooses to insinuate is too big an option to insure first-class, or true-to-type, wines.

(Please bear in mind that while the legal requirement is 51%—many vintners use greater proportions, right on up to 100%.)

I repeat, all varietals are equal in so far as their basic requirement is concerned—the 51% of one variety—but some are more equal than others. Well-made varietals, from such noble varieties as Cabernet Sauvignon, Pinot Noir, Chardonnay, Johannisberg Riesling are demonstrably superior to those from such varieties as Petite Sirah or Barbera—everything else being equal. That doesn't mean that a gifted vintner cannot very often produce wines from lesser varieties that are the equal—sometimes the superior—of wines from more grandiose antecedents.

In the Eastern states the native Delawares, Niagaras, Catawbas, Scuppernongs, etc.—and lately hybrid Chelois and Bacos Noirs, etc.—are made into varietals of those names by the same 51% (or more) formula.

Because of the success of American varietal wines and the high-powered sales pitch for them in advertising, articles, books, and by word of mouth, some European vintners have entered the lists with wines bearing "varietal" names. Where Burgundy or Chablis or Macon once covered the white Burgundy front, now we have Chardonnays and/or Pinot Chardonnays from the French growing districts of the grapes of that name. However, in the case of the import, count on 100% of the grape of the name being in the bottle.

Normally, in France, the *appéllation contrôlée* laws dictate the approved grape(s) for making any name wine and that's all. For example, if a man were to make a red Bordeaux, from the simplest regional brand to a Château Lafite, he would be limited to using Cabernet Sauvignon, Cabernet Franc, Merlot, and Malbec —with a smattering of Carminère and Petit Verdot. The proportions are up to the vintner. But should he choose to call it "Cabernet Sauvignon," then there must be 100% "Cab" in the bottle. A puzzlement, isn't it?

B. **The "Generics."** This is the largest category of the wines of the Americas—*all* the Americas. These wines use the place names of foreign strands preceded—by law—with the local geographic area name; viz., Burgundy is the French place name and California Burgundy or Argentine Burgundy, etc., is the name of the generic counterpart produced in the Western Hemisphere. "Counterpart" is used advisedly. Sometimes there is a relationship between the wine and the wine from the name region—and sometimes there is none whatsoever. For instance, Sauternes from the Bordelaise area of that name is a rich, *liquoreux* wine made from overripe Semillon and Sauvignon grapes. California Sauterne (without the final *s*) is often a dry wine, bearing no relationship to its namesake, either in taste or grapes of origin.

The French take a very dim view of our nomenclature. They have fought it without interruption—and without great success. They want to know why we can't call our California Champagne "Sparkling Napa" or "Russian River Brut." Spain says why not "St. Helena Cream" and not plagiarize her Sherry? Italy declares Chianti to be a Tuscan wine only, protected by the Italian designation of *origine*. Portugal has taken the step of calling all Ports, a name they can't protect, "Porto," a name they can. Only Cognac seems to have kept its name unscathed. It's Cognac if it's brandy from Charente—from anywhere else in the whole world, brandy is brandy.

The American vintner fights back. He says he has popularized California Burgundy, New York Chablis—made even the import of the name better known and in greater demand. He says he's

been doing it for so long, to change now would only serve to further confuse a less than educated public.

So that's the story. I can see both sides of the coin, and that's always devastating in an argument. Of late, the pendulum in other countries—England, Canada, Mexico, etc.—has swung toward the right of geographic protection. (As this is written, Bermuda has just outlawed any use of the word "Champagne" except on the wines actually coming from Champagne.) Perhaps now that the United States producer is becoming surer of himself his wines have proved their merit and value, and the United States public is indeed better informed, we shall discern a trend to a more native nomenclature.

C. The "Proprietaries." No need for a long harangue about these brand-name wines. If you know what a brand of peas or bread or cereal is, then you'll easily place such names as "Paisano" as a private label of Gallo, "Emerald Dry" as a private brand of Paul Masson. Varietal Cabernets Sauvignons or generic New York State Chablis may be made by dozens of producers; a proprietary is the sole product of a sole vintner. If you want it, you must go to that one source for it. Hence, it follows that uniformity is the prime desideratum of a brand—whether it be in ketchup or wine. It is every vintner's wish to create a private formulation that will appeal to the public and send them scurrying to *his* door, and no other, for the better mousetrap.

VINTAGE

This seems as good a place as any for a brief discussion of a subject that seems to confound so many and shouldn't—vintage.

Every grape, every vintner, every vineyard, every grape-growing area and country has a vintage every year. It may be good, or bad, or in between. The year may matter a very great deal or it may matter very little. But when a grape ripens and is picked to be made into wine—that is the vintage. To call good wines vintage wines basically makes very little sense, as *all* wines have to be born in one year or another—good and bad.

In the more northerly climes of Europe—in Germany, Champagne, Burgundy, Alsace, Bordeaux, and in the Loire and the Rhône valleys—the vicissitudes or blessings visited by Mother Nature upon the vines can vary enormously from year to year. In Italy, Spain, and, yes, California, the variations take place in much more confined limits, while in New York the Finger Lakes act as great temperature controls, keeping vintage variants to a minimum.

The nonsense that "every year is a vintage year in California" is just that—nonsense. Every growing season varies depending upon presence or absence of frost, number of degree days, moisture—deluge or aridity, and at what stage of grape development —and so on. The difference is that, in "swing" areas such as Bordeaux or Germany, one year can approach disaster, another will be "the year of the century," and still another can be so-so, with individual wines displaying considerable variation, depending upon the skill of the vintner or location within the area. A Bordeaux of 1961 will be, generally speaking, long-lived—sensational; one of 1968 is, more often than not, a complete dud; 1972 produced some good and some poorer wines, depending upon whether the grapes were harvested before or after the deluge. Recent vintages in California shaped up somewhat like this:

1968—a splendid year, long-lived
1969—lighter wines, drink now
1970—bad frosts, short crop, good wines
1971—cool weather and late spring, heavy rains, light wines
1972—frosts in spring, very hot summer, rain in September; choose carefully

1973—largest crop on record—first class

1974—huge crop of excellent quality

1975—as this is written, a smaller crop than '73 and '74 and not quite as good as the summer and early fall promised

1976—a large harvest of quality; a little early for dogmatism

I have two other vintage comments to make:

1. In white wines (and pinks too), except for certain special exceptions such as German *auslese* and *beerenauslese* wines, Sauternes, some Tokays, and a few others, drink your whites young. The cobweb syndrome, which infects most immature judgments, dictates the widespread canard that many young wines are immature. Right—but that's the time to drink 'em. This is particularly true of light, gay Californias. They're not going to improve with age; the opposite is more likely.

2. With red wines, it's just the opposite. We often drink them too young. Where a fine château won't put its wines on the market for four or five years after making, our reds are rushed to the bins after only a year or two of aging. That's why, when you do find a California red of five or six years of age, you'll likely pay through the nose for it; and beyond that, the prices escalate incredibly. Thirty dollars a bottle is commonplace for a ten- or fifteen-year-old Cabernet Sauvignon or Pinot Noir.

Masson and Christian Brothers will have no truck with vintage dates. They say it only inhibits them from blending their best wines, which may require percentages from two or more years. If a vintage date appears, it must be 95% of that year. (The 5% can be of another year and is simply a recent sop to those who must "top" or add wine to make up for evaporation from the barrels.) In Europe, the vintage dates aren't so strictly enforced except in France, and there a leeway is permitted in certain areas for the addition of wine (up to 20% tops, usually) of another year if, in the process, "the public is benefited." In California, New York, etc., the major value of the vintage date to you and me is to tell us how old the wine is.

GRAPE VARIETIES

A few words about some of the wine grapes of the Americas would seem to be in order. Chemically you would be hard put to distinguish between one grape and another, yet it is the slight variations in content, between the sugars (3 of them), alcohols (8), esters (4), acids (6), minerals (7), nitrogenous substances (3), acetaldehydes, phenols, pigments, and vitamins that account for the vast array of wines and wine tastes.

Eastern Grapes
(NATIVE VITIS LABRUSCA)

Concord—ubiquitous, strongly foxy; used for kosher sweet wines.

Isabella—used in sparkling wines and rosés.

Catawba—a widely planted white, for still and sparkling wines.

Delaware—the best of the natives.

Iona—not what it once was; a red grape making white sparkling wines.

Scuppernong—not a labrusca but a *muscadinia. rotundifolia.* The other two are the James and the *Misch*—so help me!—a Southern-state grape for sweet wines.

Moore's Diamond and **Ives** are other varieties.

HYBRIDS

Baco Noir—a French cross; successful for red wines.

Maréchal Foch—another French red cross.

Chelois, Aurora, Cascade, Seyval Blanc, Veritas, and a number of numbered grapes from Seibel are other hybrids that point to better and better Eastern wines.

Cayuga White is Geneva Station's most recent cross and has already been voted "most likely to succeed."

Western Grapes
(VITIS VINIFERA)

Red

Cabernet Sauvignon—without question, California's star performer. A wonderfully full, big wine, of astonishing longevity. The adjectival set, who look for metaphors, liken it to black currants in aroma. I am not well enough acquainted with how black currants smell to take a strong position. But distinctive and memorable it is. In Bordeaux, where this grape is the basis of most of the famous clarets (never 100%, however), splendid bottles of twenty-five, fifty, even a hundred years are not unheard of.

Pinot Noir—France's red Burgundy grape. Highly temperamental. U.S. vintners are only now learning to plant this fine grape in cooler areas and to vinify it properly.

Zinfandel—California's mystery grape—probably one of Haraszthy's importations that lost its label. Perhaps Hungarian, perhaps Italian, it is California's most widely planted grape—and here too, the vintners are learning to use it to best advantage. Varies greatly, winery to winery—from light, pinkish to strong and inky black.

Gamay Beaujolais—really a clone of the Pinot Noir. The true Gamay of Beaujolais is the Napa Gamay (or Gamay Noir), but some vintners still call its wine Gamay Beaujolais. Fruity and pleasant.

Petite Sirah (or **Syrah**)—the grape of the Rhône. Growing fast in popularity as a varietal. Robust, peppery-spicy nose, manly, usually a mixer.

Barbera—a grape of Italy's Piemonte. Can be coarse but is always sturdy and forthright.

Ruby Cabernet—probably California's most successful hybrid—for warmer climes than "Cab" will take. "Ruby" by law, must be used in conjunction with the word "Cabernet."

Grignolino, Merlot (a bit of a Martini and Sterling special), **Carignane** (a Sebastiani favorite), **Charbono** (an Inglenook special), **Pinot St. Georges** (a Christian Brothers special) are other types usually for blending but some now varietalized.

White

Chardonnay (sometimes **Pinot Chardonnay**)—California's best white wine when well made. Aroma of fresh fruit. Style not as austere as in France, where it makes the great white Burgundies. Varies widely from producer to producer.

Pinot Blanc—some call it a kissin' cousin of the Pinot Chardonnay or Chardonnay, but Pinot Blanc is not basically a Pinot at all. Its wine is not as big or as rich.

Riesling—the true German Riesling is called the White (correct name) or Johannisberg (popular name) Riesling. In California, it never achieves quite the delicacy of the best Moselles and Rhines. *Sylvaner*—not a true member of the Riesling family, called the Franken Riesling because it originated in Franconia, Germany. Does well in California. If a wine is simply labeled Riesling it is likely from the Sylvaner grape. *Traminer* and *Gewürztraminer*—especial claim to fame of Alsace though also used in the Rhineland. Very perfumed and pungent. Gewürz, meaning spicy, is a clone of Traminer and so successful that in Alsace the plain Traminer has been retired as an appellation. A "comer" in California. *Grey Riesling*—not a Riesling at all. In France it is the Chauché Gris. Makes a mild, not terribly distinguished wine. *Emerald Riesling* is a hybrid of white Riesling and Muscadelle. Makes a light, delightfully fragrant wine. One of the most successful hybrids.

Sauvignon Blanc and Semillon—these grapes are usually associated because, together, they make Sauternes (⅓ Sauvignon, ⅔ Semillon) and Graves (⅓ Semillon, ⅔ Sauvignon) in Bordeaux. In California often used separately. Sauvignon Blanc, to my way of thinking, is one of California's great successes, despite its somewhat earthy flavor. Also known as *Fumé-Blanc* and/or *Blanc Fumé*, and *Dry Sauterne*. Semillon is softer and sweeter—makes the wines often called *Haut Sauterne* and sometimes wines preceded by the word "Château," which in California connotes sweetness, more akin to the French Sauternes, although "noble rot" is seldom engendered as in Barsac and Sauternes.

Chenin Blanc—from the Loire, where it is known as Pineau Blanc de la Loire and makes such wines as Pouilly Fumé, Vouvray, and Sancerre. In California it usually is made into a somewhat sweeter wine.

Green Hungarian—the most intriguing thing about this is its name. Except for one or two producers who know how to use it, not a very distinguished wine as a varietal—better as a blender.

French Colombard—increasingly important grape. Usually a mixing or blending grape but now some varietal Colombard is available. I find it very pleasant. It can be grown from the cool North to the hot Central Valley. Obviously, then, Colombard comes in many flavors!

Folle Blanche—makes a better wine in California than it does in its native Charente, where it is grown for distillation into Cognac. Not seen too often as a varietal—Louis Martini has a sort of patent on it!

The Wineries and Wines
of California

A FEW PERSONAL REMARKS

Wine is a highly subjective matter. There is no Holy Writ. There is no black and white. Wine is not the Magna Carta. It is a (to me) highly delectable beverage that can make any meal—from meat balls to pheasant in full plumage—that much better. What I like is what *I* like. I may provide certain guidelines for you because I have tasted more wines than you. Just as a music or art or dramatic critic is in a position to judge simply because of his greater exposure and intimacy with the subject, so a wine critique of mine—or any other wine writer's—is only worth reading for its guidelines, not for pronouncements.

Another thing: the wine producer, of any country, is a highly emotional, often opinionated, and, yes, sometimes biased practitioner of the art of grape rearing and the science of wine making. Chauvinism may have a place in the market place but not in a non-aligned, free, and open discussion of one man's opinion.

I think it goes without saying that our American vintners have performed miracles in a very short time. Prohibition only ended in December 1933, leaving most vineyards torn up, foreign wine makers gone home, and a public grown used to bathtub gin. In less than fifty years we have created a billion-and-a-half-dollar phoenix from the ashes. This simply means we have an up and growing wine industry, West and East, which offers wines we can be proud of in any company, and a lot of good vin ordinaire that can hold its own with the bulk of the standard wine of the world.

To say that all United States wine is great would be as silly as saying that no United States wine is great—or, for that matter, that all French wine is great. Every country produces only so much cream at the top; the rest is milk, ranging from half-and-half to skim!

The proliferation of vineyards and wines, of late, complicates an inordinately complicated subject. Vest-pocket vineyards, whose product is sometimes not even found away from the winery much less out of state; huge deals involving the purchase of famous vineyard names by conglomerates and horizontal corporations; the development of new grapes, and recently of new blends involving Eastern and Western gallonage; new techniques both in the field and in the plant; wildly fluctuating prices for both grapes and wine—all of these, and other phenomena, have compounded the difficulties of compiling a reasonably exhaustive list of availabilities. But we are not angels—so let us not fear to tread. If the listings be treason to this man or that, to this wine or that, make the most of it. I can assure you it is all well intentioned and if it clarifies to any degree what is always a difficult subject, so that the reader can discriminate with greater facility —thereby removing some of the fear or doubt in buying—it will have served a useful purpose for all concerned. One additional word: I shall not try to paint a picture of the loveliness of California's wine country, or tell the fascinating stories of many of the historic wineries. This is a Quick Guide, and besides, one doesn't have to visit Heinz to enjoy their pickles. This, then, is a *wine* discussion and, I shall hope, a useful one. *Achtung, Attention, Hear This:*

Prices will of course vary as time goes on, but not enough to date the following statistical material by more than a small percentage.

Also, prices vary with vintage and age. No great attempt will be made to equate price and vintage, as vintages come and go. Vintage differentials are not that great in America, and old vintages are hard to come by at best. I hereby invoke the Law of Averages!

Also, the wines listed are by no means the exhaustive list of what each vintner makes. It represents those I have been able to taste and which I deem particularly worthy. That doesn't necessarily mean that unlisted wines are "not worthy"; first, I may not have had them and, second, my taste may not be yours.

CALIFORNIA WINERIES

NAPA

Christian Brothers
Napa, Calif. 94558
Estab. 1882

Run by Brother Timothy of the world-wide order—a skilled vintner and a wonderful human being. Marketed by Fromm & Sichel, affiliated with Seagram. Alfred Fromm knows and loves Beethoven as well as he does Christian Brothers wines. His brother, Norman, also a great lover of music, founded "Music in the Vineyards" in 1958. Nearly two decades later, Alfred cut the canvas, so to speak, of the San Francisco Wine Museum. Franz Sichel has passed away.

QUOTATION: "There is no such thing as a perfect wine"—
Alfred Fromm.

Christian Brothers doesn't believe in vintaging—wines are
blends of various years. Should you absolutely insist on knowing
the year of a particular bottling, refer to the number on the back
label of a Christian Brothers wine. The first two numbers tell you
the month, the third the year, the last two the day.

They do, however, have some wines that are "estate bottled" and carry a cuvée number.

QUOTATION: "Blending makes it possible to achieve better balance, uniformity, personality, and greater depth of interest and complexity"—*Brother Tim.*

They are the largest producers in Napa. (Christian Brothers is also the largest producer of brandy in the United States. Their XO brand is 50% eight-year-old pot-stilled. Excellent—in the over $7.00 class.)

WHITE

Pinot Chardonnay	$3.50	An extremely good bottle for the price, or even for more.
Johannisberg Riesling	$3.00	Very pleasant. Big nose. Fruity. Could have more body.
Pineau de la Loire Estate bottled	$3.50	Interesting. All own grapes. A bit sweet. In glass one to three years.
Sauvignon Blanc	$2.75	A nice, assertive, earthy wine of real body.
Château la Salle	$2.50	A pleasant, quite sweet, light muscat.

Cabernet Sauvignon	$3.25	Very good. Can improve quality with a year or two in glass. The one I had bottled 1973.
Pinot Noir	$3.00	Bottled 1969—the one I had. New vines from District 1 will improve future Pinot Noir.
Pinot St. Georges Estate bottled	$3.50	Huge. A triumph. Rich and big. Will go on for years. A Burgundy style.
Zinfandel	$2.50	Fruity and quite decent. A claret style.
Burgundy	$2.00	Three years in bottle. Nice nose. Pleasant.

Inglenook
Rutherford, Calif. 94573
Estab. 1879

This is part of the United Vintners complex—owned by Heublein. Once a Finnish sea captain's preserve (Gustave Niebaum), it was later owned by my friend John Daniel, who used to share steaks with me at the old railway station restaurant in Rutherford. The premium wines are Napa "estate bottled" though the vineyards are not necessarily contiguous. The secondary Navalle brand is made near Asti in Sonoma but bears the Inglenook label. Inglenook is primarily a red wine maker, and a top-notch one.

Johannisberg Riesling Estate bottled	$4.00	Vintages vary. The '72 had a lovely nose—sweetish, as a German *auslese*. 100% Riesling.
Dry Semillon Estate bottled	$2.75	Has Sauvignon in it. Popular vintages vary. Earthy.
Sylvaner Riesling	$2.75	Improves after two years in bottle. True to type of Franken Riesling.
Grey Riesling	$2.50	Not a Riesling character; more like an early-picked Muscat. 100%.
"Vintage" Chablis	$2.00	There are few vintage generics. 1972 bone dry. Growing in popularity.
Navalle Chablis	$1.75	$3.25 for the half gallon. Good for the money. Can maintain uniformity as non-vintage.

RED

Charbono	$4.25	Only producers of this as a varietal. Vintages vary. Like a big Italian wine.
Zinfandel	$3.15	Vintages vary. 100% a varietal. '70 well made.

Cabernet Sauvignon Cask bottling Estate bottled	$6.25	Aged over three years. '68 was superb. Contains Merlot.
Cabernet Sauvignon Regular	$5.15	Regular contains no Merlot—more tannic.

Recently added, a line of inexpensive District Vintage Wines (Burgundy, Zinfandel, Chablis, and Rhine—and a Grenache Rosé). Excellent values.

Beaulieu Vineyard (BV)
San Francisco, Calif. 94104
(Winery—Rutherford, Calif. 94573)
Estab. 1900

This is also a Heublein winery now—once the preserve of Georges Latour, founder, but owes most to André Tchelistcheff, wine maker from 1937 to 1973, and Richard Peterson (now with Monterey Vineyards), who succeeded him. All wines are vintaged. The reds, especially the "Cabs," are BV's glory. Not a vast gallonage enterprise and not meant to be. In October 1974, BV's Private Reserve Cabernet Sauvignon took first prize in the annual evaluation of French and California "Cabs" and clarets. There were 101 wines and the panelists were California's top vintners and critics.

WHITE

Beaufort Pinot *Chardonnay* Estate bottled	$5.00	Fermented in barrel. Complex, round, '70 was superb. Also '71, aged in Limousin oak.

Beauclair Johannisberg Riesling	$4.00	Nice Riesling smell and character. In some years, botrytis grapes add sweetness—costs more.
Johannisberg Riesling Spätlese	$5.25	Only 3000 cases in '72 but what a wine! True overripe nose and flavor.
Chablis Estate bottled	$2.75	Use only BV's grapes. Growing fast. Contains French Colombard and Chenin Blanc. Not too sweet.

PINK

Beaurosé	$3.00	Tart, not sweet.

RED

Gamay Beaujolais Estate bottled	$3.00	100% of Gamay Beaujolais—not Napa Gamay. Soft and buttery.
Beaumont Pinot Noir	$4.75	Aged one and a half years in oak. Grapes grown in new Carneros region. Picked late.
Cabernet Sauvignon Regular	$5.00	One year less in wood. More tannic. Many might prefer. Contains press wine.

| *Cabernet Sauvignon*
Latour Reserve | $6.50
and up | 100% "Cab" kept separate from Regular. Long-aged—two years in wood and two in bottle. Location of vines only difference between Latour and Regular. Vintage important in taste and price. All "free-fun." One of California's greatest wines. |

CHAMPAGNE

| *Private Reserve* | $7.50 | Disgorged with no dosage of sugar. Dry but full-bodied. On yeast, three years. A real *nature*. Delicious. |

Beringer
San Francisco, Calif. 94108
(Winery—St. Helena, Calif. 94574)
Estab. 1876

This is one of Napa's show places. The old stone Rhine House is worth seeing. The new winery is in the Carneros area. The property is now owned by the Swiss colossus, Nestlé. Myron Nightingale is the new wine maker. Count on increasingly good Beringer wines, and more of them, in the Midwest and East as distribution proliferates.

WHITE

Fumé Blanc Estate bottled	$3.25	High percentage of Sauvignon Blanc grapes—the per cent in any varietal is Nightingale's decision.
Chenin Blanc Estate bottled	$2.50	Slightly sweet but crisp.
Chablis	$2.00	Contains Chenin Blanc, Pinot Blanc, Colombard, and Semillon. Clean and dry.

Traubengold, a new white, a blend of Riesling and muscat, is being introduced at this writing. First report—high marks.

RED

Pinot Noir	$4.25	Vintages vary, so do prices. Not big.
Zinfandel	$3.00	Two years in wood and one in bottle. Non-vintage. Scores well in tastings.
Cabernet Sauvignon	$5.00	85% to 95% "Cab." Two years in wood. Tannic when young, as it should be. Always one year in bottle before release.

Barenblut (Bear's blood)	$2.75	Here is a brand, or monopole as it's called, that goes way, way back—a blend of Grignolino and Pinot Noir. Pleasant.
Malvasia Bianca	$3.25	100% white Muscat. Strong—18% alcohol.

Chas. Krug Winery
St. Helena, Calif. 94515
Estab. 1861

There are no nicer people than the Mondavis—Peter and Robert. Peter runs Krug and Robert operates his own "Mission" winery (or winery with a "mission") nearby in Oakville. It's too bad they split up, but then again maybe it isn't. This way, we have not one but two excellent sources of wine. Now, we discuss Krug; we'll get to Bob's place in due course.

Many is the happy hour I've spent in the railroad tasting car, moored on the Krug lawn, drinking lovely wines with Peter—and often with white-haired Francis Gould, the octogenarian editor of the winery's house organ, *Bottles and Bins* (which is worth asking for; it always contains a splendid recipe from his good wife).

QUOTATION: "Wine-making is like dressing little girls—each different, each charming. Every once in a while one falls in the mud"—*Peter Mondavi.*

Napa Pouilly-Fumé Sauvignon Blanc	$3.75	Aged in oak three to four months. Really dry. Good acid. 100% varietal balance.
Pinot Chardonnay	$4.50	Excellent nose but perhaps too much "wood" in the '71 100% varietal.
Johannisberg Riesling	$3.75	Superb, big wine. Quite dry. 100% varietal.
Grey Riesling	$2.75	Slightly bubbly (*pétillant*). Very good for this grape. Quite dry.

RED

Gamay Beaujolais	$2.25	Good flavor, tart and fruity. Not a big wine.
Pinot Noir	$5.00	Not especially interesting. '70 very good.
Cabernet Sauvignon	$6.50	Good dependable wine—good tannin and body.
Cabernet Sauvignon Vintage Selection		These are something special. '65 superb at $9.50. '66 big. These wines will still age.
Burgundy	$2.75	One of the best generics. Light body. Bold flavor.

Most of Krug's popular wines are bottled under the brand names CK and Mondavi Vineyards. The CK jug wines are particularly outstanding values.

Sterling Vineyards
Calistoga, Calif. 94515
Estab. 1964

Someone once said that Sterling is the kind of winery that God would have built if he'd had the money! Well, Sterling International Paper did have, and the show-place winery of Napa is the result.

You reach this Taj-Mahal-on-the-mountain by means of an aerial funicular and the view of the valley is sensational. I must have done something right because when I was there the full moon came up as I was sight-seeing. Not to be believed.

Peter Newton and Michael Stone are the dual dei ex machina.

QUOTATION from good friend *Mike Stone:* "Certainly, microclimates are vitally important. The U. of California at Davis tends to minimize the importance of soil."

The wines are sold 80% at the winery and 20% to restaurants. Very limited store distribution, but things may change. (NOTE: Intelligence—they have! Now, greater availability.)

Blanc de Sauvignon	$3.75	Avoids that earth taste of many Sauvignons. Spicy and dry.
Pinot Chardonnay Vintages	from $5.50	Vintage important here. '69 was magnificent. '71 even more so. The finest Chardonnay I have tasted except possibly for Chalone and Stony Hill.

RED

Merlot There is also a *Merlot Primeur,* one and a half months in barrels	from $4.00	About the only vineyard with enough Merlot to make a 100% varietal. Soft and gentle.
Cabernet Sauvignon N.V. and Vintages	from $4.00	Probably the only vineyard blending Merlot and Cabernet Sauvignon à la the French châteaux.
Zinfandel Vintages	$4.50	Really rich, complex, wines of breed.

Mayacamas
Napa, Calif. 94558
Estab. 1941

Only mad dogs, and an Englishman named Jack Taylor, would think of going high into the Mayacamas Mountains and proceed to resuscitate a defunct vineyard growing inside the cone of an extinct (let us hope) volcano, at the highest point for grape growing available in all Napa County! Only dear Mary, his wife, who now produces ginger peachy herbs and seasonings, would think of going along with such a project. And only a stockbroker named Travers would think of buying it from the Taylors and maintaining the old traditions of limited, but quality, production, and reducing the line to only three wines.

W H I T E

Chardonnay $6.50 to $7.00   High price, but worth it for the experience. Long fermented, long aged in new oak (two or three years in large cask, one year in small). A huge wine. The '71 will last well into the mid-seventies. The '72 now available.

R E D

Cabernet Sauvignon $6.50 to $8.00   Fabulous wines. Big and long-lived. 100% "Cab" but experimenting with Merlot for complexity. The '71 needed more age when I tasted it. The '70 was super. The extra-aged '67 is now available at $10.

Zinfandel	$6.50	I tasted the '72. The grapes were very late-picked and long-fermented and reached 17% alcohol—a phenomenon. The '68 was fabulous but that must be gone. If found, prepare to pay $10 to $12 or more.

Mayacamas claims to have distribution now in fifteen states.

Oakville Vineyards
Oakville, Calif. 94562
Estab. 1968

How could a grandson of the Dutch consul in San Francisco with the unlikely name of Wilfred van Löben Sels, who associates himself with Peter Karl Heinz Becker, as wine maker, and Karl Werner, formerly of Schloss Vollrads, as consultant, go wrong? They haven't. Theirs is one of the fastest-growing premium operations on the Coast.

W H I T E

Sauvignon Blanc	$5.00	Aggressive is the word . . . a big wine, German in style. No residual sugar. 100% varietal. I had the '71.
Sauvignon Fleur	$3.50	Contains 20% Muscat but isn't too sweet. Was '72.
"Our House" Wine Also red and rosé	$2.25	Drinkin' wines everyone likes.

	PINK	
Gamay Rosé	$2.25	Fruity and clean.

	RED	
Zinfandel	$3.75	Here's that old raspberry aroma again—what you expect from a good Zinfandel.
Cabernet Sauvignon	$7.50	The '70 was reserved for restaurants only. Some becoming available, I hear. Well aged.

Chappellet Vineyard
St. Helena, Calif. 94574
Estab. 1969

Your only problem with Chappellet is finding it. Hidden away on Pritchard Hill, overlooking the Napa Valley, is one of the most intriguing wineries in California. At first glance, it resembles one of those ultra-modern churches. Inside, everything is wide open to the high vaulted ceiling, with nothing out of place except for a few hoses snaking across the floor. Here, Donn Chappellet and his internationally trained wine maker, Phil Togni (Algeria, France, Chile, and California) are the monarchs of all they survey.

QUOTATION: "We've never bought a grape. This is a château-type operation. Every wine is estate bottled in the true sense of the word"—*Donn Chappellet.*

Chenin Blanc	$4.00	I had the '71. A bit coarse but very pleasant. Dry and very high in alcohol, 13.8%.
There is also a secondary brand—*Pritchard Hill Chenin,* made from bits and pieces of other wines.	$3.50	Pleasant.
Johannisberg Riesling	$5.00	I had the '72. Excellent, fruity, ten months in glass. Very light color—no oxidation.
Chardonnay	$7.50	I had the '70 ($6.00). Superb. Beautiful nose with good oak in taste. The '72 "will be better." 13% alcohol.
Cabernet Sauvignon	$7.50	I had the '69—round, full, big though vines are still young. 80% "Cab" and 20% Merlot. Two years in wood. Lovely wine and '70 and '71 even better.

Robert Mondavi Winery
Oakville, Calif. 94562
Estab. 1966

Bob Mondavi will turn into a grape one of these days. Never have I known a vintner who lives, breathes, has his entire being in wine making as does our Robert—former chairman of the Wine Institute and vice president of Charles Krug (his family winery, in which he is still a stockholder). With the help of a few dollars from Rainier Brewing, Bob has reared a show place—neo-colonial-style outside and 1984 within. Every new device known to wine and man is here—centrifuges, stainless steel, European oak casks, rotating fermenter—and a supply of Montrachet and La Tâche for comparison purposes!

QUOTATIONS: "To produce good wine, you need skill; to produce fine wine, you need art. . . . We are *beginning* to make good wine, to learn how to get the most out of each grape. . . . Most wine is subjected to too many treatments. . . . We get about three and a half to four tons of Chardonnay and Cabernet Sauvignon per acre, about five to six tons Sauvignon, about two and a half to three tons of Pinot Noir"—*Bob Mondavi.*

WHITE

Fumé Blanc	'70—$7.00 '72—$7.15 '73—$5.10	100% Sauvignon Blanc. Outstanding. The style is of the Loire—a *gout de terroir,* dry, fruity. I had '72. He is thinking of adding 10% or 15% Chardonnay for finesse and delicacy.
Chardonnay	$6.50	Ten months in barrel. I tried '71 and '72. Both compared very favorably with Baron Thénard's Le Montrachet, although I sometimes see no need for all this comparing. They can stand on their own.

Johannisberg Riesling	$4.50	Nice Riesling nose. Touch of sweetness which is in keeping. I had the '71.

RED

Pinot Noir	$5.25	The hardest grape to work with. Mondavi is learning. The '68 was deep and soft and the '70 more of the Pinot taste and nose. I'm afraid the Richebourg '69 comparison was too much.
Cabernet Sauvignon	$6.00 to $6.50	The "Cabs" are Mondavi's pride and joy—and rightly. This grape he has mastered. In a recent contest against "the best," Mondavi's was rated number one by his peers. The '66 was soft and big (8% Cabernet Franc); the '68 was perfection; the '70 was young and lovely and needed a little more age. The '71 was still harsh but showed real substance. '72 somewhat different technique. Deeper, fuller. '74 will be big—93% "Cab" and 7% Cabernet Franc.

There is a stunning Zinfandel '71 but only available at the winery.

Hear ye! Hear ye! Some things new have been added, wines just called:

Red Table Wine
White Table Wine

As the label says, "a wine for everyday use, made of mid-varietal and premium grapes."

Louis M. Martini Winery
St. Helena, Calif. 94574
Estab. 1940

The late Louis Michael Martini, the founder, began making wine before the St. Helena operation, so the "1940" is a misnomer. Actually 1906 is the truer starting date. Today Louis Peter Martini runs the show—and *runs* it. I remember discussing France's *appéllation* laws and their severity. QUOTATION: "I'd like to see them here try to take away my freedom. Too damn many regulations as it is"—*Louis Martini*. Perhaps so, but you have to be a Louis Martini to practice personal integrity without rules! Martini makes 33 or 34 wines. Too many, possibly, but I've yet to taste a really poor one—and Louis has learned to taste regularly, cask by cask, for special selections and outstanding lots to be separately bottled.

The appellation "Mountain" means a blend from his Sonoma and Napa properties.

W H I T E

Mountain Folle Blanche	$2.75	Said to be the only bottling of the varietal Folle Blanche. Very dry, light, popular.

Johannisberg Riesling	$3.50	Very clean and fresh. I had the '71—full of flowers and a touch of sweetness. 80% Riesling, 10% Gewürztraminer, 10% Sylvaner.
Gewürztraminer	$3.50	One of the few Gewürzes with the flowery bouquet of Alsace. I had '71.

RED

Pinot Noir	$4.50 to $5.50	I had the '65 and '66 grown in the cooler Carneros district. Both "Special Selections," both a little light.
Cabernet Sauvignon	$3.50 to $6.00	Martini's "Special Selections" are among California's glories, and always at reasonable prices. The '66 was superb and should age long and well. The '68 needed a year or two.
Zinfandel	$2.75 to $4.50	The '70 was fruity but the '68 shows what a Zinfandel can become.
Merlot	$5.00	The '68 was fine but it's scarce and hard to find as a varietal. Used to blend with "Cab."

| *Barbera* | $2.75 to $4.50 | The only competitor for Sebastiani's Barbera. Truly fine. I had the '68—superb. |

Freemark Abbey Winery
St. Helena, Calif. 94574
Estab. 1960

For a relative newcomer (the first wines were released 1967), Freemark has cut quite a swath. When such a man as learned Leon Adams says (of the Cabernet Sauvignon), "I might have mistaken it for a good vintage of Château Margaux"—and when the Chardonnay of '69 came out first in Robert Balzer's tasting—there's little more I can add except a "Well done" to Charlie Carpy, Jerry Luper, and Brad Webb.

I'm told the wines are available in more than twenty states now—among them New York, New Jersey, Vermont, Maryland—and in Washington, D.C. (Prices in the East a dollar or so higher.)

WHITE

| *Johannisberg Riesling* | $3.75 to $4.00 | A big wine with no residual sugar. |
| *Pinot Chardonnay* | $5.50 to $6.00 | They use French Nevers oak for nine months and then two years in bottle. I found the '69 sensational and the '70 even heavier—both gone now. '71 and '72 should be around—and worth searching out. |

To come, Edelwein, a 100% Johannisberg Riesling, 80% botrytis that came in at 31 degrees sugar! Incredible.

RED

Pinot Noir	$5.50 to $6.00	Light color and body. Excellent balance. Lovely bouquet. This was the '69.
Cabernet Sauvignon	$5.00 to $6.00	I tried the '69—beautiful. Twenty-two months in wood. 12% Merlot. Somebody up there knows how to make wine.

Jos. Heitz Wine Cellars
St. Helena, Calif. 94574
Estab. 1961

I had been warned to beware of Joe's sometimes testy manner. Instead of imperious, I found him warmly hosting a pre-harvest party for the Heitz "family" and I was graciously welcomed into the select circle. I think some of them could have done without me as they were kept busy fetching wines for me to taste when they could have been just partying.

QUOTATION: "We make the best we can possibly make—and we must be paid for it. We can't afford to make only *great* wines."—*Joe Heitz*.

"Martha's Vineyard" is the name given top-drawer "Cab" from a special ½-acre vineyard.

Chablis	$2.75	One of the best generics I've tasted—flinty and dry—full-bodied. No vintage. Made of Colombard, Chenin Blanc, and bits and pieces. Plenty of time to age in wood and bottle.
Johannisberg Riesling	$4.50	Spicy with a fine Riesling nose. This was the '71. The '72 was coming fine. Riesling can change radically in a year.
Chardonnay	$7.50 to $8.00	The '71 was a powerhouse but not quite ready. The '69 was big, luscious, round—one of the very best.

PINK

Grignolino Rosé	$3.00	Not at all sweet. Very refreshing, well balanced.

RED

Grignolino	$2.95	Heitz is one of the few who emphasize this grape. Does a great job with it. Interesting.

Cabernet Sauvignon	$7.75 to $11.00	The pride of the house. Five years from vintage to release. The '68 Martha's Vineyard ($11) was fantastic though the regular '68 ($7.75) was a close rival. Ditto the '67 Martha's Vineyard.

Hanns Kornell Champagne Cellars
St. Helena, Calif. 94574
Estab. 1958

Dynamic Hanns might well be called Mr. Champagne of California. His bubbly is known the length and breadth of the land. That's why I'm always a bit doubtful when they tell me he also markets some still wines. The mystery is clarified when we learn that these he selects from other wineries for bottling under the Kornell label, just as Heitz and others sell Kornell's Champagne under their imprimatur.

Kornell Champagnes are made by the *méthode champenoise* of true Champagne. The wines are bottle-fermented (in *this* bottle), riddled, and disgorged. The only variance is in the grapes used; not Pinot Noir and Chardonnay as in France, but Riesling, Grey Riesling, White Pinot, and some Semillon.

QUOTATION: "It takes a Champagne man to taste Champagne. . . . In France, you make the *cuvée* first; then the wine goes to the chemist. In the United States, the wines first go to the chemist, then we make the *cuvée*"—*Hanns Kornell.*

Champagne Sehr Trocken	$6.95	Extremely dry. No residual sugar. Not for everyone unless dry means *really* dry to you.
Champagne Brut	$5.75	An excellent, well-made wine—dry enough for me, .5% residual sugar.
Champagne Extra Dry	$5.75	Still quite a dry wine. Gold Medal at Los Angeles Fair.
Muscadelle de Bordelaise	$5.75	Slightly sweet, with the bouquet of the Muscat grape.

Kornell's Sparkling Burgundy received the "Gold" at the international competition in Milano, Italy.

Schramsberg Champagne Cellars
Calistoga, Calif. 94515
Estab. 1862

The "Established" is a little misleading. While Jacob Schramm set up shop around 1862, what we mean by Schramsberg dates from 1965 when Mr. and Mrs. Jack Davies took over.

Davies is one of the few California wine makers who earnestly believe in the French idea of world-wide distribution. No matter how small the enterprise and limited the production, France wants a few bottles of it available around the world. So do Davies and Schramsberg. Despite the high price, highest in California for sparkling wines, Schramsberg can indeed be found around the land and other lands—even to China, where the then President Nixon is said to have regaled Mao with it.

QUOTATIONS: "The French A.C. laws took a long time. I believe we will strengthen our 51% law and our 'estate-bottled' requirements. . . . We get 165 to 175 gallons of juice per ton of grapes. That's 150 gallons of wine—about 750 bottles. It takes two and a half pounds of grapes per bottle. If these grapes are Chardonnay, that means there's a dollar's worth of grapes alone per bottle—and nearly seventy-five cents in taxes"—*Jack Davies*.

Blanc de Blancs	$7.75	Excellent. Made in the traditional Champagne manner with the traditional Champagne grapes—plus some White Pinot. I had the '69. Obviously it had spent a long time on the yeast in the bottle. Three years, I'm told—then six months resting after disgorging.
Blanc de Blancs Reserve Cuvée	$8.75	Splendid. More Chardonnay in this and longer aging. Perhaps the best bottle in California. I had '68.
Blanc de Noir	$10.00	A rarity. A Champagne from a preponderance of red Pinot Noir grapes. Wonderful nose of Brut. I had '68. (In 1970, for the first time, this wine in magnum.)

Crémant $6.75   This one not as Brut as all
                          the others. More an Extra
                          Dry style.

Soon, a "Cuvée Nature"—a still wine from the *cuvée* used for the Blanc de Noir. This is to celebrate ten years of operation.

Souverain Cellars
Northcoast Cellars
Geyserville, Calif. 95441
(Also in Rutherford, Cal. 94573)
Estab. 1943

Begun by Lee Stewart and developed by him into one of California's best, it once became a Pillsbury bake-off. No longer. Biggest claim to fame was the making of Green Hungarian into a 100% varietal. They also are using the relatively new hybrid Flora, love child of the Semillon and Traminer. The new Château Souverain is a Sonoma facility—now producing only premium varieties. Souverain recently won a scad of medals in San Francisco at a very top-drawer "experts'" tasting.

Chablis	$2.50	Nice and dry and somewhat like a Muscadet.
Flora	$4.25	A very pleasant new taste experience.
Green Hungarian	$3.25	Cheers for a reasonably flavorful wine from a usually pallid grape. '71 was very good.
Pinot Chardonnay	$6.00	Price is on the steep side but the wine is worth it. '70 excellent.

R E D

Zinfandel	$4.25	Good Zinfandel raspberry overtones.
Cabernet Sauvignon	$6.50	Steep but worth it. The '68 was fantastic.

Spring Mountain Vineyards
St. Helena, Calif. 94574
Estab. 1968

Relatively new, relatively small, definitely great—that's Mike Robbins' new venture. His vineyards are only coming into bearing in toto but, my, what he's done with some of the other fellow's grapes! Not widely available.

Chardonnay $5.50 to $7.50   The $7.50 is for '69, one of the greatest Chardonnays yet produced in California. It's the price for '72 too, which I haven't tasted.

R E D

Cabernet Sauvignon $6.50 to $9.00   High price? Sure—but wait until you try the blend of '68 and '69. '70 very big, and complex.

Stony Hill Vineyard
St. Helena, Calif. 94574
Estab. 1951

Don't think you're going down to your friendly neighborhood wine shop and bring home a bottle for dinner tonight. There are only about 1000 cases made *a year* and Fred McCrea, a onetime ad man, accounts for quite a bit himself. I remember, years ago, stopping at an unprepossessing shop in St. Helena and being touted onto a bottle of Stony Hill Chardonnay which I carted back to San Francisco for dinner. Mirabile dictu! What a wine. I thought then, and I'm not at all sure I still don't, that it was the finest bottle of white I'd ever tasted in California.

W H I T E

Chardonnay $6.00   I don't remember the year of the bottle mentioned above but the '71 is mighty good—and not overpriced.

Gewürztraminer	$4.25	Crisp and spicy as it should be.
White Riesling	$4.50	Clean and flowery, beautifully balanced.

Stony Hill produces 600 half bottles each year of Semillon de Soleil—a wine made from grapes sun-dried in trays, the way Italian Vino Santo is made. For what it is and the scarcity, $6.00 for '71 and '72 and $8.00 for '70 doesn't seem too high for such nectar.

S O N O M A

Korbel
Guerneville, Calif. 95446
Estab. 1886

The world, and living in it, were both simpler when Korbel just made sparkling wines and that was that. In those days the three Brothers Heck were pleased with me for declaring the Korbel Brut about the best California Champagne I'd tasted. It was. The Hecks invented a mechanical riddling machine and automatic disgorging so that they could say "fermented in *this* bottle" just as it's done in Champagne itself. But the demand of the trade became too strong, so in 1965, Korbel opted to offer a whole line of "stills." With Jack Daniel's as distributor, what would *you* do? I don't condone but I don't condemn, even though it's against the way I'd like to see California go—toward specialization rather than proliferation. However . . .

WHITE

All the Champagnes, especially the *Brut* and drier *Nature*—excellent. $5.80 to $6.75

Sonoma Blanc $2.30   A blend of "mountain" grapes. Slightly sweet.

Chablis $2.15   Clean, light, mainly Colombard and Pinot Blanc.

Dry Sauterne $2.30   No connection with a Sauternes but pleasant.

(I haven't tasted the new *Chardonnay*.)

Château Vin Rosé $2.15   Not as sweet as the word
"Château" usually
connotes.

RED

Burgundy $2.25   A good blend for the price.

Pinot Noir $3.75   Has a roundness. 85%
varietal.

Cabernet Sauvignon $3.75   Has a true "Cab"
character. 80% varietal.

Zinfandel $2.75   Fresh and young.

I haven't had a chance to taste them, but you will: in the fall
of 1975, Korbel launched a Johannisberg Riesling and a Chardonnay—breaking a ship over each bottle! Quite some steps for
the ol' Champagne makers. Oh, heck.

Sonoma Vineyards (Tiburon Vintners)
Windsor, Calif. 95492
Estab. 1970

(Windsor Vineyards is a name retained for sales by mail in
California—primarily for individualized name labels.)

If that doesn't confuse you, it does me. It goes like this: once
upon a time a fellow named Rodney Strong opened a tasting
room in Tiburon, across the bay from San Francisco, to sell
wines he had selected from hither and also from thither. Enter a
fellow named Friedman, who said, "Personalize the label so it
reads 'made especially for George and Clara,' and George and
Clara will buy." They did. Then in 1971, a huge new winery,
2700 acres under varietals, and the new name Sonoma—plus a

few headaches and problems into the bargain. These have been partially absorbed by Renfield, now a co-owner. Probably no winery has shown such consistent improvement in quality. Their very latest offerings are truly sensational but are being marketed just too late for this book. Seek and thou shalt find.

QUOTATION: "Wine people should make wine—not accountants or lawyers"—*Rodney Strong.*

WHITE

Chardonnay '74 Estate bottled	$5.00	A big, big wine. Just enough wood to accentuate and not jump out at you. '73 excellent, too—crisp, rich.
Johannisberg Riesling '75 Estate bottled (If you're lucky, you may also find a Johannisberg Riesling Auslese, made when botrytis strikes—$5.00 plus.)	under $5.00	Harvested early. No botrytis. From the Le Baron vineyard. Bottled early. Only 10% alcohol. Like a dainty Moselle.
Grey Riesling	$3.50	Not my favorite grape or wine, but this is a good one—on the sweeter side.
Chablis	$2.29	A straightforward, no-nonsense bottle at a right price.

New! A Brut Champagne (Cuvée ⚒ 104)—"fermented in *this* bottle" of 100% Chardonnay. Held two years. .06 sugar (between a Brut and a Nature). $8.29. Excellent.

Vin Rosé $2.39   Drier than most and with a
There is now a special   nice fruity bouquet.
Spring Rosé each year
—a blend of Gamay
Beaujolais and French
Colombard. $6.99 in
California. Sort of a
Rosé Primeur.

RED

Burgundy $2.29   A simple wine but very
                        drinkable.

Zinfandel '73   under $5.00   A sensational Zin without
Estate bottled   the heaviness often found
(bottled November   in this wine. Long in wood.
1975)   Long on skins. Long-
                                  lasting.

Pinot Noir '73 Estate bottled	under $5.00	One of the very best from this difficult grape. From the River East vineyard—Cool Zone ♯1. Intense varietal flavor. Aged in wood 16 months. Superb.
Cabernet Sauvignon	$3.50	Has "Cab" character. Nice tannic quality.
Cabernet Sauvignon	$6.25	A big one. Will last—1970 vintage superb.
Petite Sirah	$2.90	Well balanced. Excellent use of this grape.

Flash! A new line of vintage-dated varietals *in magnum*. Fantastic values: Ruby Cabernet, Fr. Colombard, Grenache Rosé, Zinfandel, Chenin Blanc—$4.99.

Sebastiani Vineyards
Sonoma, Calif. 95476
Estab. 1904

You don't just like August Sebastiani, you love him—for August is a lovable kind of man. Never out of his striped overalls, seldom out of his Jeep truck (which I think he has specially made without springs), August is a gentle, kindly man—except when women wearing heavy perfume show up at his tasting rooms! He has also transformed a big, mass producer of generics into a respected source of the best varietals. His winery is his life—except when he is feeding his birds, of which he has hundreds in his famous aviary, or collecting duck decoys and carvings, of which he has thousands!

QUOTATION: "There is no substitute for bottle age. My wines get a year in glass after four in wood"—*August Sebastiani.*

70

Green Hungarian	$2.29	One of the few who has made a huge success with this wine, more intriguing in name than in taste. 85% varietal.
Pinot Chardonnay	$3.50	Excellent Chardonnay nose. '72 vintage very pleasant—and the price is right.
Johannisberg Riesling	$3.50	A little sweet but fruity and big.

Burgundy	$2.15	I wrote down "hearty" in my notes and picked it number one.
Burgundy Vintage	$3.75	'67 is the one I had. Splendid, complex, big. Half the price of Cabernet Sauvignon.
Gamay Beaujolais	$3.00	The one I tasted was a true "Nouveau," one and a half months old. Spritely. I picked it number two.
Pinot Noir	$3.50	Big and full flavored.
Pinot Noir Special Bins and Vintages	$5.00	Vary but big and sound.
Cabernet Sauvignon	$4.00	Non-vintage has a big "Cab" nose and mature flavor.

Cabernet Sauvignon 1967	$7.00	Only released in March of 1973—over five years in wood. Longest aging in industry? Great.
Barbera	$3.00	If August had made no other wine, this would be glory enough. Big, full, tannic—what a Barbera should be.
Barbera Vintage	$4.75	Softer, more aftertaste. Smooth. This was the '67.
Zinfandel	$2.29	Good "bramble" flavor. It was my number three choice.
Zinfandel Vintage and Special Bins	$3.75	Examples of what bottle age can do to smooth out a wine.

UNITED VINTNERS
San Francisco, Calif. 94107
Italian-Swiss Colony
(Estab. 1881)
Petri
(Estab. 1933)
Léjon

If you're confused after reading this, be comforted. So am I! It's all too big. Just imagine, Gallo and United Vintners produce more wine than all the other California vineyards put together. Gallo is number one and United is number two. Heublein controls United Vintners, as of 1968, but is in a legal hassle seeking to divest it of some of its companies because of restraint of trade, or some such. At any rate, if greater detail concerns you, Joe Vercelli at P. O. Box ⚹ 1 in Asti can fill you in.

This huge combine produces more different kinds of wine than you can shake a stick at—if shaking sticks is your cup of wine. The following are a handful that I preferred over others. Remember, the prices are low—and even lower in half gallons and gallons.

QUOTATION: "Too often wineries wait too long to pass along the advantages of increased planting and large harvests to the consumer. The 'Colony' is committed to making the results available to the consumer in the form of distributive varietal wines at everyday, affordable prices"—*Bob Rife,* wine maker.

WHITE

Rhine	$1.25	Not too sweet—pleasant.
Rhineskeller	$1.25	For those who like sweet wine. A trio—Chianti (red), Grenache Rosé (pink), Rhineskeller (white)—all sweet.

Chablis		A trio of slightly *spritzig*,
Gold	$1.25	simple wines. Very popular.
Pink	$1.25	
Ruby	$1.25	

RED

Burgundy	$1.25	Simplistic. Not too much
Claret	$1.25	difference between the two.
Zinfandel	$1.35	Has true Zinfandel character. Very big seller.
Tipo Chianti	$1.99	Has a real "fiasco" style of light, tart Italian wine. Regular Chianti is sweeter and $1.25.

The biggest news on the horizon is the recent introduction of a new line of Colony (Italian-Swiss Colony) varietals, at prices hardly to be believed:

Cabernet Sauvignon		Made mostly from the
magnum	$2.99	"Cab" grape grown in the
fifth	$1.69	North.

Also, Barbera, Ruby Cabernet, French Colombard, Chenin Blanc (Zinfandel and Grenache Rosé have been in the line right along). Same incredible prices.

Probably the lowest-priced varietals in California.

Then there is a huge assortment of "pop" and specialty wines: Annie Green Springs (Trio: Peach Creek, Berry Frost, Maraschino), all for $1.00; Bali Hai with tropical fruit, Vin Kafe with coffee at 20% alcohol ($2.49), a sparkling wine by Léjon at $2.99, and a Heritage line of popular California semi-varietals such as Ruby Cabernet, Grenache, Colombard, Zinfandel, etc.

Simi Winery
Healdsburg, Calif. 95448
Estab. 1876
(present operation estab. 1970)

Russel Green (no longer with Simi) pumped more than wine there when he acquired the old winery in 1970. He pumped in enthusiasm, the legendary Tchelistcheff as wine maker-consultant, Robert Stemmler as wine maker, and the largest planting of Cabernet Sauvignon in Sonoma. That all this has succeeded I learned at first hand when my wine class at the "Y" voted Simi their favorite wines of the evening. Appellation "Alexander Valley" is an approved declaration of origin on certain Simi bottlings.

Flash! Simi is now a Schieffelin operation.

WHITE

Johannisberg Riesling	$3.50 to $4.00	True to the grape—big and aromatic. Took the Gold at the Los Angeles Fair and in Milano, Italy.
Gewurz Traminer	$4.00	Spicy and spritely (not a misprint—that's how they spell it.)
Chardonnay	$4.50	Superb. Cold-fermented. Eight months in small cooperage. Ten months in bottle. I had the '73.

Rosé of Cabernet Sauvignon	$3.25	Very successful. Gold Medal in international competition at Milano, Italy.

RED

Burgundy	$2.00	A little thin but good drinkin' wine.
Carignane	$2.50 to $3.00	Novelty. Carignane not usually bottled as a varietal. I had '71. Spicy. Big nose.
Zinfandel	$3.00	More body and lots of fruit. Quite complex.
Cabernet Sauvignon	$4.00 to $4.50	A best buy at these prices. Gold Medal at Los Angeles Fair. I had '70—quite ready. My "Y" wine class voted '72 their numéro uno.

Parducci Wine Cellars
Ukiah, Calif. 95482
Estab. 1931

Mendocino is the northernmost wine county of California and Parducci is its prophet. They make their reds without fining or filtering, so pour gently—or decant.

French Colombard	$2.50	A touch sweet. Won the Silver at the State Fair and put Parducci on the map. I enjoyed the '70.
Flora	$2.40	There's that girl again—good, too.

RED

Cabernet Sauvignon	$4.25	On the light side—but nice "Cab" nose. '69 was good.
Pinot Noir	$4.50	Also light, but will age nicely. I had the '69.

Pedroncelli
Geyersville, Calif. 95441
Estab. 1927

This is another of those operations that began as a bulk producer and became premium wine makers under later owners.

WHITE

Chablis	$2.00	Without pretension but very pleasant.

PINK

Zinfandel Rosé	$2.00	They say this is the first rosé to be made from 100% Zinfandel. Dry.

		RED
Zinfandel	$2.50	A steal at this price.
Cabernet Sauvignon	$3.50	In and out but getting more *in* than *out*.

Geyser Peak Winery
Geyserville, Calif. 95441
Estab. 1934

Recently purchased (1972) by the Schlitz people, who make you-know-what. Now, to make Geyserville famous, they are offering "Voltaire" varietals and "Summit" jugs. The Chardonnay, Pinot Noir, Cabernet Sauvignon, and Johannisberg Riesling ($3.50) were matched by the Zinfandel and Chenin Blanc at $2.50. Burgundy, Grand Rosé, and Chablis at $1.69 are also the jug-fellows, ($3.29, half gallons) but not for long—White Riesling, Napa Gamay, and "Cab" are coming in half gallons. Imagine, at $4.49. It's a little soon to judge things.

As we go to press, the "Voltaire" label is being phased out. It's "Geyser Peak" all the way. Also, a new Rosé of Cabernet Sauvignon has been added. Splendid, too.

Hanzell Vineyards
Sonoma, Calif. 95476
Estab. 1950

Here is a rich man's plaything that paid off. Mr. James D. Zellerbach—paper tycoon, financier, and ambassador—wanted to know if wines comparable to Le Montrachet and/or those of the Domaine de le Romanée Conti could be made in California. Armed with the best of enological advice, unlimited cash, and a steadfast will, he built Hanzell, planted its vineyards and—praise be—limited its production to just two wines: Chardonnay and Pinot Noir, both Burgundy types. Today the operation is no longer owned by his widow. Hanzell still makes just the two types but what were $6.00 bottles are now $8.00 bottles. If you can latch onto a Chardonnay at any price, do so. It is probably the most European of American wines—big, full, complex, and smelling of the oak of Nevers. The Pinot Noir is not as outstanding.

SANTA CLARA

Paul Masson
San Francisco, Calif. 94111
Champagne Cellars
Saratoga, Calif. 95071
Estab. 1892

One of the finest names in California—large compared to many of the vineyards; small if compared with Gallo or United Vintners. Otto Meyer, retired, its long-time president and my dear friend, is one of the most respected men in the wine business. His "nose" is legendary. As we go to press, veteran wine man Art Palombo is jumping into the Masson saddle. Masson, a Seagram operation, offers some of the best values in town. The newest Pinnacles property is producing some splendid premium wines. No vintages are used.

Masson is the only California winery to ship to the world market—seriously. Today there is distribution in fifty countries abroad. I remember offering their wines at a tasting in London eight or ten years ago—much to the great André Simon's pleasure.

QUOTATION: "Our wines must go abroad to enhance their reputation at home"—*Otto Meyer.*

Pinot Chardonnay	$3.25	Good nose. Remarkable for price.
Pinot Blanc	$2.95	One of the very best made from this grape. I gave it a Misch first prize.
Johannisberg Riesling	$3.00	Rich. Good Riesling bouquet.
Chenin Blanc	$2.50	Sweet. Becoming very popular.

(All varietals are 60% to 80% of the name grape.)

Chablis	$2.00	Excellent for price. A bit thin.
Emerald Dry	$2.15	Excellent. One of the very great "brand" successes. Uses Emerald Riesling, a hybrid grape.
Rhine Castle	$2.15	Quite sweet. Thin, fruity.

ROSÉ

Vin Rosé Sec & *Paul Masson Pink*	both under $2.00	Sweetish. Often a bit *pétillant*.
Crackling Rosé	$3.50	Quite bubbly. Pays Champagne tax. Really a Champagne. Faintly Muscat flavor. Growing.

Pinot Noir	$3.00	Good depth. Big nose and body. Lots of wood.
Pinnacles Pinot Noir	$5.00	Fine, big wine. Heart-shaped, numbered bottles—handsome.
Zinfandel	$2.50	Fruity.
Cabernet Sauvignon	$3.25	Possibly the least expensive "Cab" in California and one of the best.
Pinnacles Cabernet	$5.50	Sold only in California. Aged two–three years in wood and one–two years in bottle. Heart-shaped, numbered bottle.
Burgundy	$2.00	Well made. Deep.
Gamay Beaujolais	$3.00	Pleasant.

PROPRIETARIES

Baroque	$2.00	Aged a long time in small cooperage. Lacks a little in complexity.
Rubion	$2.00	Fruity. Claret-like. Popular. From Ruby Cabernet hybrid.

SHERRY

Rare Cream & *Rare Dry*	$3.25	A *flor* sherry. Very, very good.

Rare Souzão Port $3.25   Lots of wood aging.
                                     Excellent.

C H A M P A G N E

Brut, Extra Dry, $5.00   A very decent bottle.
and Pink

Masson Blanc de Pinot is claimed to be the first Champagne in the United States to use the approved Champagne grapes: Pinot Noir, Chardonnay. Any rebuttal, Schramsberg?

Mirassou Vineyards
San Jose, Calif. 95121
Estab. 1854

One of the founders of the industry. The sons of the fifth generation are guiding the ship. The company buys no outside wine and few outside grapes. Once a California sleeper, now being marketed nationally and aggressively. Label explains whether the wine is from Santa Clara or the newer Monterey vineyards. "Harvest" is a name reserved for the *tête du cuvée* or "best in show."

W H I T E

Pinot Blanc $3.75   Includes some Sauvignon
                                     Blanc. Aged in both French
                                     and American oak.
                                     American is the better but
                                     little is produced. A superb
                                     wine.

Monterey Riesling	$3.50	Semi-varietal;
Regular bottling	$1.75	semi-proprietary contains Sylvaner and French Colombard—25%.
Johannisberg Riesling	$4.75	A big wine, not too sweet.
Regular bottling	$2.45	Has the bouquet of late-picked grapes.
Gewürztraminer	$4.75	"7th Harvest"—7th picking.
Regular bottling	$2.20	Aromatic, excellent balance.
Chenin Blanc	$3.50	Sweet. 2.5% residual sugar.
Regular bottling	$1.75	Big hit. The '71 I tried was excellent, ditto '73.

ROSÉ

Petite Rosé	$3.00	Contains Grenache and Petite Sirah—fruity and fresh and not too sweet. Popular.

RED

Gamay Beaujolais	$3.50	All from Napa Gamay.
Regular bottling	$1.75	Fruity. Popular.
Zinfandel	$3.50	Huge success. Complex.
Regular bottling	$1.75	Tannic. '67 was fine.
"Late harvest"	$14!!	
Cabernet Sauvignon	$5.50 to $6.50	Prices vary depending upon vintage—so do the wines.
Regular bottling	$2.75	The '68 was superb.

Brut	$7.00	Well made, truly *brut*.
"Au naturel"	$7.00	
"Late disgorged"	$10.00	On yeast two years.
—1969		

Almadén Vineyards
San Francisco, Calif. 94111
Estab. 1852

If Almadén had done nothing else but show fellow vintners the meaning and value of proper and stylish labeling and bottling, that might have been enough. For this, the late and beloved Frank Schoonmaker deserves a lot of the credit. While hardly a graphics man, his interesting and informative label copy proved an inspiration to those who were. Schoonmaker was a wine man and a shrewd judge of American taste. With Louis Benoist's dollars and Schoonmaker's acumen, Almadén turned to the making of Grenache Rosé, which led the way to America's love affair with pink wines; to Sherry made with Palomino grapes, *flor*, and

the Solera Process*; to sparkling Blanc de Blancs, not such a switch, as Californians seldom bother with black grapes in Champagne anyway. Result, Almadén became, and is today, the leader in volume in the production of premium wines and fancier jugs. Almadén makes a small percentage of vintaged, estate-bottled wines. As it was explained to me, "Special Selection" means a regular wine *selected* to be aged longer and to carry a vintage date. Regular wines are N.V.

As of 1967, Almadén is the preserve of National Distillers.

WHITE

Johannisberg Riesling	$2.65 to $3.75	The '71 I tried was full of flowers, delicious; the '72 even more so.
Regular bottling (Recently I had a late harvest 1975 Riesling, just redolent of botrytis. Fabulous.)	$2.65 $5.95	
Pinot Chardonnay	$3.75	I tried the '71. Real varietal nose, light body. Excellent at price.
Blanc Fumé	$2.50	A good earthy Sauvignon Blanc of aggressive style.

* In this book, we are primarily interested in "table wines"; Sherry is a *fortified* wine, which means brandy has been added to reach about 17% to 20% alcohol. "Flor" is a process whereby a yeast is grown to film the surface [sometimes submerged] to impart a special nuttiness. A "Solera" is a system of superimposing rows of casks, one on top of another. New wine goes into the topmost row. Matured wine is drawn from the bottommost when needed for bottling. Each row graduates to the row below as times goes on.

Pinot Blanc (100%) '74	$3.25	Crisp. Brittle.
Gewürztraminer (100%) '74	$3.25	A big solid wine just now on the market.

PINK

Grenache Rosé	$1.99	Who needs to be told about this, America's darling? Refreshing and so drinkable.

RED

Grenoir	$2.25	A red, though a light-colored one. Name is from Grenache Noir. Light body. Gold Medal at the California State Exhibition.
Cabernet Sauvignon	$3.75	A little light for "Cab." My notes read "young yet." It was Special Selection 1970. Almadén has over 7000 acres in Cabernet Sauvignon.
Cabernet Sauvignon '73	$4.50	This one a Special Selection. A huge, meaty, long-lasting wine.
Petite Sirah '74	$2.25	Easy drinkin'. Best value in town.

Blanc de Blancs $6.50   One of the best bottles of Champagne made in California. The regular Brut and Extra Dry are $5.25—good too but without quite the finesse.

DESSERT

Solera Flor Fino Sherry $1.99   Remarkable for this price.
  Other Sherries and   Remarkable anyway. A
  Ports—same price.   slick, dry 17% Sherry and you can taste the *flor*.

New wines:
  Mountain Red Chianti
  Vintage Barbera
  Service Ace Solera Sherry—in, so help me, a tennis racquet-shaped bottle.

<h3 style="text-align:center">Chalone</h3>
Soledad, Calif. 93960
Estab. 1966

I've never had the good fortune to climb up Mount Chalone (or to meet Dick Graff, who runs the show). But the mountain came to Mahomet. The Chardonnay is worth the $10 tab if any bottle is. Sensational is the word—huge, oaky, full, rich. It was '69 and I was told the price was about the same for the '73. The Pinot Noir of '69 must be one of the greatest, if not *the* greatest, in California—$9.00 to $10. 1970 and 1971 Chenin Blancs were awarded "3 stars" by *The Connoisseur's Guide to California*

Wine—the only wines out of seventeen so honored. They called them "immense," rich, and luscious. I haven't been lucky enough, yet, to taste.

If you have the money—and the patience to seek it out—and the good luck to find a bottle of Chalone—you may begin to find out what California can do.

Novitiate of Los Gatos
Los Gatos, Calif. 95030
Estab. 1888

The Jesuit Fathers, in keeping with the vinous traditions of the Church, have operated this winery for five decades, turning out wines for sacramental use (two thirds) and commercial wines (one third.) Plans are in being for extending the distribution of the commercial wines and, for the first time, bringing them out from under that bushel by means of promotion.

There is a group of generics—Burgundy, Dry Sauterne, Chablis, and the sweet Château Novitiate—at $1.99; another group of quite pleasant varietals—Cabernet Sauvignon, Pinot Noir, and Johannisberg Riesling—at $3.75; and a large selection of fortified desserts: Sherries, Ports, Muscats, and Malvasias at $2.19 to $2.69.

Ridge Vineyards
Cupertino, Calif. 94025
Estab. 1962

This prestigious vineyard has outgrown the "boutique" sobriquet. It is a full-blown winery, high up in the Santa Cruz Mountains, operated by the "six professors," giving Ridge Wines the highest I.Q. on the market. I've not been fortunate enough to taste the entire line but the Zinfandels and Cabernet Sauvignons I have had are *very* top drawer. The "Cab" '71 was luscious, big and fruity ($7.50, I believe—other "Cabs" go much higher: $21 for '68 and '70; $14 for '67 and $10.50 for '65.) Zinfandels are distinguished on the label by place names explaining what vineyard they're from; viz., Lodi Zinfandel '72/'73, $3.75; Geyserville Zinfandel '70, $5.25; Mendocino Zinfandel '71, $4.75, and '72, $4.20. Zinfandel Essence '72 (made from sun-dried raisin-like grapes 14½% alcohol), $11. '73 Riesling and Chardonnay, Vine Hill, are $5.00; Monte Bello is $6.75.

A new Vine Hill White Wine is an interesting and quite complex everyday white wine—a blend of years—$3.50.

Martin Ray
Saratoga, Calif, 95071
Estab. 1958

Way up on top of Mount Eden, Martin Ray, enfant terrible, taught the industry some valuable lessons—viz. that 100% varietal does make a difference, that making a few wines well is better than just making a lot of wines, that dispensing with filtering and fining can often leave a wine more complex and interesting. What put Martin Ray on the map was the effrontery of charging $50 a bottle for a '70 Chardonnay. Eight to ten dollars will get you Chardonnays today and well worth it, too. The Pinot Noir I also found superb because I like a big, powerhouse of a red. Martin Ray also made a few special sparkling wines. His Blanc de Noir, from Pinot Noir red grapes, is quite remarkable—if $20 a bottle is no objection! The Martin Ray "property" has recently been divided—and the new ownership and the new setup are too complicated for me, and probably not of earth-shaking import to you.

ALAMEDA

Weibel Champagne Cellars
Mission San José, Calif. 94536
Estab. 1945

One of California's oldest and best-known wineries, especially for sparkling wines and sherries. Weibel table wines coming up strong. Weibel does a big business in private label. One of the few wineries that uses both the *flor* process and a Solera system in making their sherries. In the making of their Champagnes, Weibel uses the Charmat or "bulk" process for private label and "transfer" for their own. (See the chapter "A Little Background.")

QUOTATION: "All wine is a continous series of decisions. . . . Over the years wine men develop individual styles in wine"— *Fred Weibel.*

WHITE

Pinot Chardonnay	$5.75	Estate bottled. Grapes from own, contiguous "estates." I enjoyed the '69.
Green Hungarian	$2.50	Most popular varietal. People like its semi-sweetness. No complexity. Easy to drink.
Chardonnay Brut Champagne	$7.50	Blanc de Blancs, non-vintage. Truly *brut*.

RED

Cabernet Sauvignon	$6.00	Vintaged. Aged a year in tank, two months in small cooperage. 90% "Cab."

Pinot Noir	$5.50	Vintaged. 100% Pinot Noir. Excellent nose and heavy body. Not too tannic.
Burgundy	$1.90	Soft. Pleasant bouquet.

SHERRY

Dry Bin Cocktail	$2.25	Not too dry. Good *flor* nutty taste.
Amberina Cream	$2.25	Sweet—4.5% sugar. Pleases many.

QUOTATION: "We couldn't *sell* a true .8% Fino dry"—*Weibel*.

CORDIAL

Tangor	$2.99	A 20% alcohol blend of wine, brandy, and flavors. Orangy.

Llords & Elwood
Los Angeles, Calif. 90035
Estab. 1933

That 1933 is a bit of a misnomer. That was when Prohibition ended and Mike Elwood opened a chain of wine and liquor stores in southern California specializing in wine. It wasn't until 1961 that the first Llords & Elwood wine appeared. Today the business is operated by Richard Elwood, Mike's son. And—sh-sh! —there never was a Llords—just sounded nice.

L. & E. are very big in fortified wines, and very good at it. Their table wines—varietals—are now coming on. So is Eastern distribution: New York, New Jersey, Washington, D.C., and Atlanta first.

FORTIFIED

Great Day Dry Sherry	$3.50	Extremely dry, perhaps the driest in California. No cooking. Casks aged in open-air as in Jerez. Very good. 100% Palomino grapes. Aged an average of three and a half years.
Dry Wit Sherry	$3.50	Not quite so dry—style of Dry Sack of Williams & Humbert.
The Judge's Secret Sherry	$3.75	A cream sherry—60% Palomino and 40% Pedro Ximinez grapes—style of Harvey's Bristol Cream.
Ancient Proverb Port	$3.50	The proverb: "Take a little wine for thy stomach's sake." 100% Quito Madero grape. A ruby, and not too sweet.

WHITE TABLE

Chardonnay	$4.25	Still in the more or less experimental stage but going to be a fine wine.
Castle Magic Johannisberg Riesling	$4.25	Big, full wine—medium sweet.

PINK TABLE

Rosé of Cabernet	$3.50	Also big in style. A little sweet. Nice.

RED TABLE

Cabernet Sauvignon	$4.25	None are vintaged "to maintain uniformity." Soft and complex.
Pinot Noir	$4.25	Also soft in style—tannin low. A wine for cheese.

Wente Bros.
Livermore, Calif. 94550
Estab. 1883

I can still remember Herman Wente, with his big boots clop-clopping about the office—whence he seldom came! He was a vineyard man. Karl is the boss man today, he and charming Mrs. Karl. He can no longer be called the Lord of Livermore because now the Wentes have added a big chunk of vineyard land down Monterey way. Eighty per cent of the grapes Wente uses are their own, I'm told, and with a 650,000-gallon annual production that's a lot of grapes. The Wentes have always specialized in white wines and are best known for them—and for sensible prices, always.

WHITE

Grey Riesling	$2.50	Wente's best seller. It has more zip than most of the bland Grey Riesling, thanks to 25% Sylvaner no doubt.
Château Semillon	$2.75	Used to be Ch. Wente. A sweeter wine but with good varietal characteristics. Supposedly patterned after Ch. d'Yquem.

Dry Semillon	$2.50	I had the '72. 100% varietal. Very pleasant. Dry. Estate bottled.
Sauvignon Blanc	$2.75	Estate bottled '72. Fresh and refreshing.
Chablis	$1.99	My notes read: "Very darn nice for the price, combines Pinot Blanc and Chenin."
Pinot Chardonnay	$3.50	The '71 was big and full. 100% varietal. Excellent even at twice the price. 90% Livermore, 10% Monterey. They say the '70 was even better.
Blanc de Blancs	$2.50	A blend of Chenin Blanc and Ugni Blanc. Grapey.
Riesling Spätlese Special Selection	$6.50	Have been called "Best whites in U.S." Small
Riesling Auslese Special Selection	$6.50 .	production—late-picked of grapes attacked by *Botrytis cinerea* as in Sauternes. '69 sensational. None left. '72 and '73 flowery, rich.
Gewürztraminer Special Bottling	$4.50	Small production. Peppery and pleasant, but not a true Gewürz. I had '72.

PINK

Rosé Wente	$1.99	Two-thirds Grenache and one-third Gamay. Not entirely dry, but pleasant.

Zinfandel	$2.50	You won't need the price because most all goes to American Airlines. The '69 was excellent.
Pinot Noir	$3.25	Estate bottled. From Monterey, with Carneros. Velvety. I had '70.
Petite Sirah	$2.75	100% varietal. A very good bottle, the '70 I had will age.

Concannon Vineyard
Livermore, Calif. 94551
Estab. 1883

Joe and Jim Concannon do a fine job down Livermore way. Starting as producers of altar wines—their father did, that is—they have branched out into wines for general use and vie with neighbor Wente for the championship of Livermore Valley. Some years ago they began producing special, small-quantity "Limited Bottlings" which, while uneven, can only be described as outstanding. I have my own little hieroglyphics to characterize wines in my notebooks. I find an unusual number of notations for "excellent"—for instance:

WHITE

Chablis	$2.50	Big nose, excellent deep taste. Their biggest seller.
White Dinner (There's also Red Dinner)	$1.90 Gallons $7.50	Very good carafe wines—all Livermore grapes.

Moselle $3.00   One of the few wines by this name in California. Contains Chenin Blanc, Grey and White Riesling. Nice bouquet.

Sauvignon Blanc $3.50 to $4.50   The '72 was a good bottle but the '71 "limited" had great depth and big body.

PINK

Zinfandel Rosé $3.00   A rosé for people who don't drink rosés. Dry and with character.

RED

Petite Sirah $3.50 to $8.50   One of Concannon's glories. Introduced in '64. '65 sensational. '70 very good, big, cherry-like. '68 good. They use this grape well.

Cabernet Sauvignon $6.00 to $11.50   That $11.50 is for '65—gone but not forgotten. '67 very good and '68 is splendid. Contains some wine from Hallcrest, one of California's best vineyards, now Concannon-owned.

Prelude Dry Sherry $2.95   This is primarily a
                                             table-wine book but this
                                             Sherry deserves mention.
                                             60% *flor,* I'm told, and
                                             reputedly "driest in
                                             California." 17% alcohol.

In case you have an old price list, 1893 for instance, which I
perused, you might want to order Concannon Claret at $3.25 per
case and Burgundy at $3.75 a *case.* Sherry was $1.25 to $3.00 a
gallon, by the barrel. Brandy was up to $5.00 a gallon and Zin-
fandel grapes brought $5.00 a ton!

SAN JOAQUIN

Franzia Brothers
Ripon, Calif. 95366
Estab. 1933

This is another of those huge affairs that leave me gasping. Franzia is said to be fourth producer in California. There is a
profusion of labels and monopoles. Only the name "Ripon"
identifies them as Franzia-made. The prices are low enough,
goodness knows; $1.00 to $2.00 for fifths; $2.00 to $3.00 for half
gallons; $3.00 to $4.00 for gallons. I found the wines on the
bland side and I think that's because they are catering to the
least educated palates among us with soft, sweetish wines.
Family-owned, the company "went public" a few years ago, so
you can buy either the stock or the wine. Of late, it has been
acquired by—of all people—Coca-Cola.

Chablis Blanc	$1.19	Somewhat coarse, but drier than most.
Rhinewein	$1.09	Not very Rhenish. Not very good. But very popular.
Champagne Extra Dry	$1.99	Imagine such a price—and I'm told it's made by the Charmat process. You'll be as surprised as I was at its unpretentious quality.

PINK

Grenache Rosé	$1.29	Pleasant enough. One of, if not *the,* lowest-priced varietals on the market.

RED

Zinfandel	$1.29	Ditto.
Chianti	$1.09	No characteristics of its namesake but drinkable.
Burgundy	$1.19	Ditto.

A whole new direction is planned for Franzia's wines in a new shape "teardrop" half gallon for premium/varietal introductions including Robust Burgundy, Chablis Blanc, and Grenache Rosé as well as a group of generics and sparkling wines.

East Side Winery
Lodi, Calif. 95240
Estab. 1934

A very large farmers' co-op, this one, producer of the wine and brandy that made East Side (East Side of Lodi, that is) famous —Royal Host brand. As you would expect, they make a zillion wines. I found the Gold (from a new hybrid) and Grey Riesling very acceptable, especially at the $1.99 tab.

Guild
(Winemasters', Cribari, Vino da Tavola are Guild labels)
(Cresta Blanca—Estab. 1882—and Roma are wholly owned)
Lodi, Calif.
San Francisco, Calif. 94111
Estab. 1962

This is California's largest grower-owned co-op, representing 10% of all the grapes crushed in California. (Incidentally, you snobs, no cause for surprise. Co-ops are big in Europe, representing 65% of all wines produced. In Bordeaux they are said to represent 30% of all; in Germany, 35%.)

Guild's Winemasters brand is to be the flagship of the line, and—here's a switch—it will appear on both California premiums and a new lot of imports from France, Germany, Italy,

and Spain, as well. The most expensive are a Barolo from Italy at $6.50 and a regional Pauillac (Bordeaux) at $6.00; the least, a Rosé d'Anjou and a Valpolicella at $2.70. That late-lamented, dependable taster and editor, Charles van Kriedt, says the Pauillac is "worth it" and a German Riesling at $3.70 was his "first choice."

Flash! Cribari's latest is Vino Fortissimo. It is! Deep in color, heavy-bodied, 14% alcohol (jugs only).

Guild is important also in brandy. The trade names are Ceremony and Guild. In 1966 the weather was so propitious, Cresta Blanca made probably the first *vintage* brandy in the United States—$7.00. Even Cognac doesn't do that!

Guild has a huge line of California table wines under the same Winemasters' label:

Dry Semillon, Chenin Blanc, Grenache Rosé, Green Hungarian, Blanc de Blancs	at $2.15
Pinot Noir, Cabernet Sauvignon, Gamay Beaujolais, Petite Sirah, Johannisberg Riesling	at $2.80
Chianti, Burgundy, Rhine, Sauterne, Pink and Gold Chablis	at $1.50
Ruby Cabernet (new, and good)	at $2.00

From Cresta Blanca and Roma I selected these:

WHITE

Cresta Blanca French Colombard	$2.50	Excellent. Not too sweet. Shows what a Colombard can be by itself.

Just introduced (1974) a batch of new Cresta varietals all made under cold fermentation: Gewürztraminer, Pino Chardonnay, Green Hungarian, Johannisberg Riesling—and a dessert Muscato di Canelli.

		RED
Roma Burgundy	$1.35	Good generic for the price.
Cresta Blanca Petite Sirah	$2.75	Gutsy. Good tannin. Plenty of tank age—more than most.
Cresta Blanca Zinfandel	$2.75	Nice Zinfandel raspberry nose. Rated fifth among all in *Time* poll.

		PINK
Cresta Blanca Grenache Rosé	$2.25	Dark—almost a light red wine. Dry, and with some tannin.

DESSERT

Cresta Blanca also produces some excellent Sherries—especially Dry Watch, Triple Cream, and Palomino Pale Dry—and a two-year-old Tawny Port. The Triple Cream won the rare Grand Prize at the 1974 Los Angeles County Fair. A Souzão Port is a new arrival; also Fin de Nuit—Cresta's first proprietary. It is a Sherry with natural flavors added.

CHAMPAGNE

The Extra Dry Champagne was a Gold Medal winner at the Los Angeles County Fair. At press time, Cresta Blanca announces a new White to meet the burgeoning demand for whites: Cresta Blanca Blanc de Blanc, $2.00, plus a few cents.

MONTEREY

Monterey Vineyards
Estab. "Yesterday!"
(First crush—Fall 1974)

This is an absolutely fabulous new operation and underlines
Monterey as a number-one California grape-growing area. Ten
thousand acres are nurturing the best varietals, in Monterey for
"Monterey." Miles of overhead, and the newer ground-level irrigation pipes are turning an arid valley into the most talked-of
new vineyard property in California. This spanking new winery
was just having its lid put on when I was there. Several months
later I tasted the first wines. Incredible what can be done—and
so soon. The future is boundless for these first-class wines at a
price anyone can afford.

WHITE

Chardonnay	$4.50	Sensational for a wine from such young vines. Rich and elegant and the price is low for such a wine. I had '74, natch—the first crush.
Chenin Blanc	$3.00	Fruity. A touch of becoming sweetness but crisp.
Del Mar Ranch	$2.75	Contains Chenin Blanc, Pinot Blanc, and Sylvaner in a blend likely to become everybody's everyday wine.

I also had a Johannisberg Riesling that was sensational—wine
with a real "noble rot" lusciousness. Not in general distribution
but worth seeking out. My favorite. $4.25.

Gamay Beaujolais	$3.25	Light, gay—easy, not *grand sérieux*.

The reds are being given more time to develop before being released, as I write this.

MODESTO

Gallo Vineyards
Modesto, Calif. 95353
Estab. 1933

It's a bit presumptuous to think I can tell you anything about Gallo that you don't already know. For Gallo=Wine to most of the U.S.A. Doing a third of the total wine business of California (175 million gallons), Gallo is not only a household word but a household product.

> Breathes there the man with soul so dead.
> Who never to himself hath said,
> This is my own, my native brand?
> *R. J. Misch, age 10*

Operating their own glass plant, buying more grapes than anyone else in California (probably in the world), hiring the finest technicians the world's enology centers can produce—the wines of Gallo may be inexpensive but they are never cheap.

I remember luncheon with Ernie (I have not had the pleasure of meeting Julio) and his lovely wife (a great cook, incidentally). With the pasta, Ernie circled the table, slicing fresh white truffles onto each plate. In front of each person was a cluster of five Baccarat crystal goblets. The wines were Gallo!

It would be impossible to catalogue more than a very small proportion of the huge array. The big news is the recent entrance of Gallo into the varietal field with some remarkably good bottles selling for about the $2.00 mark.

WHITE

Chablis (also "pink")	$1.19	Remarkable. Clean, fresh, well made.
Rhine Garten	$1.19	On the sweet side, but not cloying.

PINK

Vin Rosé of California	$1.19	Pleasant. Quite dry.

RED

Hearty Burgundy	$1.19	The wine that made the Gallos famous. The way people drink it, you'd think a gallon was a miniature.
Paisano	$ .99	A little sweet, perhaps, but I prefer it to the Burgundy.

And latest, *Tickle Pink*—get it?

There are also vast numbers of "pop" and "mod" wines that began with the milestone Thunderbird and followed on with Ripple, Boone's Apple, Spañada, and such—and a Champagne, originally called Eden Roc but now just Gallo Champagne. Pretty darned good, too.

The new *varietals*—French Colombard, Chenin Blanc, Riesling, Sauvignon Blanc, Zinfandel, Ruby Cabernet, and Barbera, absolutely outstanding in the $2.00 range. The Barbera, Sauvignon Blanc, and Zinfandel were my favorites.

CUCAMONGA

Brookside Winery
Guasti, Calif. 91743
Estab. 1952

This is an unusual operation. The wine properties are about the most southerly in California, yet thanks to the mini-climates in Cucamonga and in the new Temecula (Rancho) district, cooling winds permit the growing of good varietals. Brookside is the creation of the French family Biane and a great job they've done. Instead of bringing you to the vineyards they've brought the vineyards to you—setting up over thirty tasting and selling "rooms" all over California and as far away as Arizona. Assumption Abbey and Vaché are two of their other brands. Today the whole operation is owned by Beatrice Foods of Chicago.

WHITE

Johannisberg Riesling Assumption Abbey	$2.75	100% varietal. Nice nose. Light body.
Malvasia Bianca	$1.50	A varietal. Sweet, perfumed, but quite interesting.

| *Emerald Riesling* | $2.50 | Not quite dry, but mellow and pleasant. |

PINK

| *Mouvedre* | $2.50 | A dry varietal rosé. Interesting. |
| *Fiesta Rosé* | $1.50 | Sweet—from a Sangría base. |

RED

Dido Noir	$2.50	$3.50—half gallon. $6—gallon. The Carignane in it softens it in aging. Nice.
Petite Sirah	$2.75	From the newer vineyards.
Zinfandel	$2.50	Good bouquet, pleasantly tannic.
Cabernet (Ruby Cabernet)	$2.75	A big dry wine but not astringent.

NOTE: The volume wines are labeled Brookside Cellar Wines. From young new vineyards: were $1.00, fifths; $1.65, half gallons; $2.70, gallons—a bit more now. Chiantis, Sauternes, Chablis, etc., fortified wines—under $2.00

OTHER VINEYARDS

RIVERSIDE

Callaway Winery
Temecula, Calif. 92390
Estab. 1974

This small but fascinating new enterprise is the creation of Ely Callaway, retired head of Burlington Industries. I rush to inscribe these few words as I have only just tasted a few of the firstborn and must indicate surprise and pleasure. Scarce, but worth searching out.

NAPA

Stag's Leap Winery
Napa, Calif. 94558
Estab. 1970

I wish I could tell you more about this superb small winery, but it is relatively new and I've only tasted a very few of their excellent wines while this book was already far along. First crush was 1973.

SONOMA AND MENDOCINO

Foppiano Wine Co.
Healdsburg, Calif. 95448
Estab. 1898

A family enterprise for decades—now spreading out with increased distribution. Once a tank-car operation selling bulk varietals. Zinfandel is well made and I liked the Petite Sirah. "Russian River" is often on the label.

Buena Vista Winery
Sonoma, Calif. 95476
Estab. 1860

Many's the happy hour I have spent lolling in the gardens of this, the winery established by the famous Count Haraszthy himself. I didn't loll with the Count but with old friend Frank Bartholomew, newsman (United Press) turned vintner. What a lovely host—what a dedicated winesman, if there is such a word. The hours he spent trying to wean me to Green Hungarian. He never succeeded. The Zinfandel and Cabernet were more to my liking—and still are. He sold out in 1968 to Young's market, who, bless them, haven't tried to make it huge. Such a great name should be cherished.

Hacienda Winery
Sonoma, Calif. 95476
Estab. 1973

Welcome back to wine making, Frank Bartholomew, after five years (since he sold Buena Vista). This will be no colossus either (15,000 gallons) and will concentrate on Chardonnay and Cabernet Sauvignon and a few other varietals. (No comment on the wines as I have not had an opportunity to taste, but with Frank B. you can't go wrong.)

Joseph Swan Vineyards
Forestville, Calif.
Estab. 1969

This small vineyard deserves mention if only for the fact that *The Connoisseur's Guide to California Wines,* not much given to exaggeration, selected its Zinfandel for "3 stars." It is $4.00 a bottle. The only other 3-star Zinfandel was Ridge's 1971 Mendocino ($6.75). The Vintners' Club picked it second only to Cresta Blanca.

Grand Cru Vineyard
Glen Ellen, Calif. 95442
Estab. 1971

An interesting small newcomer specializing not only a splendid Zinfandel but the newfangled Zinfandel white! They even offer a Zinfandel "Nouveaux" made by carbonic maceration.

Russian River Vineyard
Forestville, Calif. 95436
Estab. 1964   Reorg. 1975

This is a brand-new operation in the Russian River area. First crush, a very worthy Zinfandel, offered in 1975.

Fetzer Vineyards
Ukiah, Calif. 95482
Estab. 1968

A small "hobby" operation to start—now a respected small winery of quality. The Zinfandel is superb, and of late the Mendocino Cabernet Sauvignon and Chardonnay are listed right up there with the greatest that California produces.

ALAMEDA

Davis Bynum
Albany, Calif. 94716
Estab. 1965

I never got to taste the whites but the red Charbono and Petite Sirah were very good wines, and the Zinfandel better than that. My favorite among wine names is probably "Barefoot Bynum." Try that on for size—the size, half gallons and gallons. The

"Private Reserve" name is reserved for exceptional limited editions.

SANTA CLARA

David Bruce
Los Gatos, Calif. 95030
Estab. 1964

Dr. Bruce is a dermatologist who prefers dealing with *Botrytis cinerea* to acne. He makes some of the best wines in California. They are not cheap: $4.00 to $12 these days, but his '69 Chardonnay hit $22. Today he offers a '71 at $12 and a '71 Pinot Noir at from $7.50. Zinfandel ranges from $5.50 to $7.50 for Late Harvest, to $9.00 for Essence (an experience); Cabernet is $8.50 for the '72, which ain't hay. Bruce wines are well worth tasting but you'll have to hunt. Only a few selected outlets stock them.

San Martin Winery
San Martin, Calif. 95046
Estab. 1892

An oasis (but hardly a watering place) on the road between Los Angeles and San Francisco. Generics begin at $1.99 and go to "Cab," Pinot Noir, and Pinot Chardonnay at $3.50. Try the Pinot Noir first. But, for a surprise, their exclusive Malvasia Bianca is a Muscat that's sweet but not cloying; ditto the new Moscato Canelli ($4.00 in California) made by cold fermentation . . . golden and fragrant. This wine won a Gold Medal in Amsterdam's thirteenth annual World Selection of Wines and Alcohols. The Johannisberg Riesling '74 took a Silver. Right now the winery is experimenting with a new wine—"Soft Chenin Blanc"—a 100% varietal of only 9% alcohol. "A new German process," they call it.

SAN JOAQUIN

Bear Mountain Winery
(M. Lamont)
Arvin, Calif. 93203   Lamont, Calif. 93241
Estab. 1969

I know these wines best under the M. Lamont name and was more than pleased at the low prices for some of the varietals offered. Formerly the Di Giorgio property, Keith Nylander has taken over and is doing a job that should make the line a winner. $1.59 for the generics but the varietal French Colombard, Barbera, Zinfandel, Emerald Riesling at $1.99 are real buys. My notes tell me that the Emerald Riesling and the Colombard tied for the Misch first prize. If you like a huge Cream Sherry, they have a Black Monukka that's something special.

Ficklin Vineyards
Madera, Calif. 93637
Estab. 1945

Walter Ficklin, Sr., a gentleman I had the great good fortune to know, was a man after my own heart—a "specialist." Feeling the Central Valley was right for the true grapes of Oporto, he planted Souzão, Tinta Madeira, etc., and proved it by making— and still making—the finest Ports of California, and probably the only vintage Ports in the state.

California House Wine Co.
Campbell, Calif. 95008
(Producing Winery, Papagni Vineyards, Madera, Calif.)
Estab. 1973

Remember the old adage: "Sell the sizzle, not the steak"? That's what these people are doing. They offer Burgundy, Chablis, Rosé, Zinfandel, Chenin Blanc, and Sangría in—get this—4.9-

gallon "collapsible and disposable Saran-lined dispensers made of 500-lb. test double wall corrugate." No, I don't quite understand it either but it seems the liner is filled in a vacuum so it collapses as the wine is drawn, keeping out air and preventing oxidation. Should be a great thing for a restaurant's carafe service—no more vinegarization of the leftovers in jugs. What will they think of next?

P.S. Valley Rouge Wines of Winnipeg, Canada, is launching a "me too," but theirs is a gallon plastic bag inside a box. The bag collapses as the wine is consumed as in the above. The whole container weighs less than four pounds. It was to debut in California in 1975, so perhaps it already has. I also understand that Almadén has two "casks" of this type in distribution.

Giumarra Vineyards
Edison, Calif. 93220
Estab. 1922

This is a huge shipper of fresh table grapes, lately decided to get its feet wet in wine. Cork closures and, at an under $2.00 tab, the bottles (unique in design) will carry both varietals (Petite Sirah, Zinfandel, Barbera, Green Hungarian, French Colombard, Chenin Blanc) and generics (Burgundy, Chablis). I found them splendid for the price. So, evidently, did the judges at the Los Angeles Fair in '74. Giumarra won two Golds (Cabernet Rouge and Petite Sirah), a Silver, and a Bronze.

KERN COUNTY

California Wine Association
Burlingame, Calif. 94010
Estab. 1953

A rather confusing setup, this. At one time, a huge conglomeration of "eleven cellars." Over the years, centrifugal force flew them apart. Today the names used are Ambassador, Guasti, and Fino Eleven Cellars. The Burgundy, Claret, and Chianti at under $2.00 are excellent buys. "Best buys," in varietals are the French Colombard and Barbera. There are also Sherries, Ambassador Vermouth, and Aristocrat and famous Morrow brandies. At the helm, to this day, is nonagenarian Antonio Perelli-Minetti, a graduate of the Royal Academy of Viticulture and Enology at Coregliano and one of our most respected vintners since 1902. He has recently patented a new grape variety, Perelli 101. It will only be marketed when Antonio Perelli-Minetti feels it is "ready." Preliminary tasters call it spicy, gutsy, high in tannin, gingery in taste.

SOME ADDITIONAL WINERY LISTINGS

Acampo, Barengo, Bargetto Winery, Bertero Winery, Bisceglia Bros., Bonesio Winery, Butte Creek, Burgess Cellars, California Growers, Chateau Montelena, Chateau Vintners, Cambiaso, Caymus Vineyards, Cuvaison, Delicato, Dry Creek, Edmeades, Filice, Fortino Winery, Franciscan Vineyards, Gavilen, Gibson, Husch, Los Altos, Lyncrest, Matthews, Martini & Prati, Montevina, Nepenthe Cellars, Nichelini, Pedrizzetti, Pesenti, Joseph Phelps, Nave Pierson, Pirrone, San Antonio, Sherrill, Sutter Home, Trentadue, Veedercrest Vineyards, Vina Vista, Woodbridge, Yverdon.

To my vintner friends:

I'm sure I'll be more censored than pitied—by wineries left out (remember the time factor), by wineries that feel they should have more than a mention, by wineries that disagree with my opinions. I know how it feels to work very hard and have someone underrate, omit, or damn by faint praise. Please believe me, the compilation of a book such as this is hard work too—and just as you make a mistake now and then, in planting "Cab" where

Zinfandel should be, or in fermenting too long or too little, or in blending X with Y when Z would have been preferable, find it in your heart to forgive me for errors of omission and/or commission. (Also, remember prices change without warning—as do wines. These also often vary in price and quality in traveling from winery to East Coast.)

R.J.M.

CODA

A Conversation at Davis

("Davis"—School of Enology of University of California at Davis. I spoke to a Prof. Anonymous. I do not want either the responsibility of misquotation, revealing an off-the-record opinion, or dealing with a possible change of mind).

HE: "There are many micro-climates; each one is right for a certain variety(s) of grape. In general, Semillon and Sauvignon and Cabernet Sauvignon are the best grapes for the California latitudes.

"Burgundy varieties are not right here. In Burgundy, the growing season is short but the days are very long and the sun is never directly overhead. The day length is as important as the temperatures during the day.

"For good wine you need: the right location for the type of grape, ten-year-old vines, devoted vineyardists, and devoted enologists for the fermentation, processing, and aging. The whole operation is about twenty years in duration.

"Soil has an important but secondary effect on grapes. In Europe, they have a high proportion of phosphates and limestone in soils that are no good for vegetables or fruit trees; only grapes grow well. On poor soils, crops are small and wines taste better because the grapes develop more flavor elements."

ME: "Why, in France, is Montrachet so much better than its hyphenated neighbors, just across a wagon road?"

HE: "It could be due to differences in freedom from virus or it could be differences in the subsoil. Masson and Almadén are trying phyloxera-free, ungrafted plants. Such cuttings are cheaper and save two years in grafting and vine growth. In sandy soil, vines grow roots faster than the louse can chew them off."

ME: "What does California do that's different from the Spaniards in making Sherry?"

HE: "The best of Californias now produce *flor* or a film of yeast cells. In Spain this lies atop the barrel for years and keeps air from wine. Here, we agitate and mix in the *flor,* submerge it, and get flavor in a few days. In sweet Sherries, alcohol is too high for *flor* and so the wine is oxidized and tastes entirely different. Another thing, a real Solera—one barrel on top of another feeding down—would take twenty years or more to establish and be prohibitively expensive. In Spain they were set up generations ago. Things didn't cost so much then."

ME: "Do the vintners of California produce too many wines?"

HE: "Yes. California is still 'new' and searching for proper viticultural regions, an optimum grape for each area, only since 1933. Note Hanzell (only two wines), Freemark Abbey (only four wines), Stony Hill (only three wines). It's the distributor who wants the 'full line.' Give us two more generations of vines (fifty years) and we'll have made more progress in the direction of right grapes to the right area. Fifty years will see great changes. The United States is today the world center for the study of virus diseases. We are producing new and better grape varieties and hence getting better wines: Emerald Riesling, Ruby Cabernet, a new one—Carnelian—and B-12, even better (not released yet). Ten years from now, the children may be better than the parents."

The Wineries and Wines
of New York

NEW YORK—''WE'RE NUMBER 2''

New York, the Empire State, is second only to California in the production of wine—a very modest second but still second. New York produces about 25 million gallons of wine a year of which better than a fourth is sparkling wine.

No other state, or country for that matter, can claim so high a percentage of bubbles to still wine; no other state has had such a running skirmish with the drys of the Women's Christian Temperance Union; no other state exacts such high fees for wineries, had an Episcopal priest as a wine maker, or uses all three grape varieties—labrusca, vinifera, and hybrids—in the making of its wines.

New York is second to California in wine consumption too—22% for California to 13% for New York of the national 100%. (Illinois and New Jersey are a poor third and fourth.) The D. of C. is, per capita, ahead of them all, for that matter, and so is Nevada, but they're special cases.

The states with the lowest adult wine consumption are Iowa (the lowest), Alabama, Kentucky, and West Virginia. Is that good?

A FEW HISTORICAL NOTES

When Leif the Lucky and his fellow Vikings first sailed down the coast of the North American continent, it wasn't the Golden

Gate they saw but the shores of Newfoundland and the Maritime Provinces of Canada, and possibly New England. To their astonishment, grapes were growing in profusion, despite the rigors of the climate. Vineland is the name they gave to what was probably Newfoundland.

They say some French Protestant refugees who had settled in the Hudson Valley (Ulster County) were the first to domesticate the vine. That was in the late 1600s.

They, and many after them, tried to grow the familiar wine grapes of Europe—to no avail. Harsh winters took their toll, and kept on doing the same with recurrent plantings right down to the twentieth century. But in 1818 a Baptist deacon in the Chatauqua country on the shores of Lake Erie successfully planted enduring native varieties, especially the Concord. In 1829 an Episcopal minister, William Bostwick, whom many regard as the father of the New York State industry, planted Catawbas and Isabellas in what is now the wine capital of New York, Hammondsport on Lake Keuka, one of the Finger Lakes. Strange, isn't it, how often the names of churchmen recur in the history of viniculture, especially strange in upstate New York where a combination of the W.C.T.U., rigid rural churchgoing communities, and various and sundry Prohibitionists fought wine grapes— every cutting, stake, and vine—along the way?

The final major area, Niagara County, joined the Hudson, Chatauqua, and the Finger Lakes about 1840. But it was in the 1860s that things vinous really began in New York with the advent of the Pleasant Valley Wine Co. (Great Western) near Hammondsport. To this winery goes the honor of making the first New York Champagne. That was 1865. Today, the Finger Lake area produces a third of all New York's grapes but over half of them are used for wine. (The majority of vines grown in the other areas yield table grapes or juice.)

In 1880 a cooper by the name of Taylor arrived in Hammondsport. Instead of sticking to his last, or to his hoop, he went into the wine business. In 1961 the Taylors bought their neighbors down the lane, Pleasant Valley, and the Taylor-Great Western axis is the colossus of the East. They produce over 15 million gallons of wine, 800,000 cases of Champagne annually—the largest outside of California. Not too long ago the company "went public."

A handful of other wineries: Widmer's, Canandaigua, Boordy, Bully Hill, O-Neh-Da, Niagara, and the Hudson River group represent the New York industry. Brief descriptions follow, but one important event should be chronicled here. In 1882 the Geneva Experimental Station was established. Geneva is to New York what the Enological School at Davis is to California's vintners and industry. It is not an integral part of a university, as Davis is to the University of California setup, but it does have important working arrangements for students at Cornell University, itself situated "far above" a Finger Lake. Geneva works with grape varieties, viticultural developments, hybridizing, and the like—even makes experimental wines (good ones, too).

THE GRAPE PROBLEM

No discussion of Eastern wines continues very long before the words "foxy," "labrusca," "hybrid," and "vinifera" crop up. Let us dispel any mystery forthwith.

There are two *major* grape families: *Vitis vinifera* (the grapes of Europe and their descendants planted in California, South

and Central America, Canada) and *Vitis labrusca* (the wild grapes of the Eastern states.) The latter are hardy, withstand severe winters, and are impervious to the devastating root louse, (phylloxera). Most vinifera do not and are not. Hence the hybrid—a cross between hardier American types and/or root stocks of selected vinifera grapes. The hybrids, some originating in France and some here, are being planted more and more where labrusca once held sway. Straight hybrids, or some hybrids added to the blend, are changing the New York flavor scene. Some people love the "foxy" (grapey) taste of straight labrusca. Some do not. For these, the hybrids and, more recently, some Eastern-grown true vinifera, are the answers.

If you can please all of the people some of the time, and some of the people all of the time—you'll do all right in the wine business!

THE GRAPES

The labruscas primarily used:

Concord (somewhat improved for wine from the familiar purple slip-skin you squirt across the table); Isabella (used primarily for Champagne types); Catawba, Delaware (perhaps the best); Diana (Widmer makes the only varietal of this); Dutchess; Elvira and Noah and Diamond (not much seen any more).

The hybrids:

Baco Noir ✕1 (better here than in France where it originated); Foch (they say it's foolproof); Seyval Blanc (from the Seyve-Villard 5276); Chelois (pronounced Shelloy); and no less than five Seibel numbered crosses—for instance, Aurora (Seibel 5279).

''AMELIORATION''

Labrusca grapes are very high in acid, and the labrusca taste and smell can be intense. Hence, vintners are permitted by law to "ameliorate" by adding up to 35% water and sugar (they never add one without the other). The vintner decides how much but must report to authorities. It does not appear on label. Some companies are now incorporating low-acid California wine for the same purpose. This whole practice of chaptalizing (e.g., adding sugar to the crush) is explosive in wine-making circles. I shall take a discreet position firmly on the fence.

THE WINERIES

Taylor-Great Western
Hammondsport, N.Y. 14840
Great Western—Estab. 1860
Taylor—Estab. 1880
Taylor-Great Western—Estab. 1961

If you take a look at their annual report (which, while a joint report, is entitled simply "The Taylor Wine Co., Inc.") you'll know these people must be doing something very right. Doing a business in excess of $52 million annually, increasing at a far greater pace than the national percentage of increase, crushing over 16,000 tons annually, producing 24 products under the Taylor legend and 31 called Great Western, perhaps the philosophy of the company is sound: viz., to make products people can afford to buy, especially the under-thirty-five young adults, who drink five times more wine than the over-thirty-fives!

GREAT WESTERN:

Baco Noir	$2.25	All French hybrid—no labrusca. Good nose. A little sharp.

Chelois	$2.25	60% to 75% of the Chelois "varietal." Mellow. Ages less quickly than Baco.
Isabella Rosé	$2.25	Labrusca but little foxiness. Pleasant.
Diamond Chablis	$2.25	Labrusca and some hybrid. Not much body.
Aurora	$2.25	This varietal name takes over from "Sauterne." Sweet.
Special Reserve Champagne	$5.15	Not quite *brut*—well made.

(Great Western recently won Bronze awards and the comment "very good" from the Club Enologique of England, in competition with wines of six countries, for their Diamond Chablis, Baco Noir, and Special Reserve Champagne.)

TAYLOR:

Rhine	$2.00	Delaware and Aurora. A touch sweet.
Chablis	$2.00	A nice, crisp, dry, tangy wine; a favorite of mine.
Claret	$2.00	Labrusca plus hybrids. Thin.
Lake Country White	$2.00	Niagara primarily. A bit sweet. Highly popular.
Lake Country Pink (There's also a *Lake Country Red*)	$2.00	Catawba predominates. Nice nose.

Ruby Cabernet	$2.25	Soft and fruity—a varietal with California wine predominating.
Taylor Brut Champagne	$5.00	Quite dry.
Taylor Regular Champagne	$5.00	A little sweetness. Popular.

A relative newcomer—Keuka White from Ontario, a Geneva Station hybrid. Fruity. Light in color. Also, to honor '76 in 1976, Taylor offers a very limited-edition Champagne for—you guessed it—$76.

Gold Seal
(Formerly Urbana Wine Co.)
Hammondsport, N.Y. 14840
Estab. 1934

Of late, Gold Seal and Charles Fournier (born to the grape and the bubble in France's Champagne district) have become practically synonymous. Charles, president of Gold Seal and my dear old friend, is today semi-retired (but you can't keep an old fire dog away from a fire), is in a major way responsible for the growing of the vinifera in the state of New York. It seems that

a certain Dr. Konstantin Frank, born in a German enclave in the Ukraine, had had the task of raising vinifera grapes in weather conditions as rigorous as those in New York. When the war uprooted him, he and his wife came to this country. He found his way, somehow, to the Geneva Experimental Station where Charles Fournier met him and offered him a job initiating a vinifera program at Gold Seal, where they said it couldn't be done. This was 1953. No easy task. He had to train workers in grafting. He had to find suitable root stock. He had to find the most propitious locations for the vines of Riesling and Chardonnay. In 1961 he left Gold Seal (he and Charles Fournier are still good friends and true believers) to start his own vinifera winery but his work lived after him. Today Gold Seal is extending his vinifera plantings and is bottling straight vinifera—not a lot, but an ever increasing quantity—and is using vinifera to supplement Gold Seal hybrids and labruscas.

WHITE

Chablis Nature	$2.35	Fruity and mellow. Soft and pleasing. Contains Riesling and Chardonnay. One of the Misch "best buys."
Chardonnay	$3.25	Very little of these two
Johannisberg Riesling (Once in a great while, a *spätlese* when the "noble rot" occurs)	$3.25	100% varietal viniferas is made but be on the lookout—an experience.
Rhine Wine	$2.00	A bit sweeter but very pleasant. Contains Johannisberg Riesling for style.

RED

Burgundy $2.35   Comes closer to what is
                                      meant by a Burgundy than
                                      most who use the name.
                                      Hybrids predominate.
                                      Fermented on skins.

Labrusca Red $1.69   No pronounced labrusca
                                      nose—quite a pleasant
                                      drink, even for labrusca
                                      haters. Hot press for color.

PINK

Catawba $1.89   The star! Mellow and
                                      vinous. Remains on the
                                      palate. The
                                      Catawba—probably a
                                      labrusca cross with some
                                      long-forgotten vinifera. 5
                                      million cases have been
                                      sold!

CHAMPAGNE

Chas. Fournier Blanc $6.50   Superb! Made by transfer
   de Blancs   process. No riddling.
                                      Pressure filtration. Long
                                      aged. In 1950, won the
                                      Sacramento (Calif.) State
                                      Fair Gold Medal. Since
                                      then, outsiders are not
                                      invited to the fair! How do
                                      you like that?

Gold Seal New York State $5.25   A very well-made bottle.
   Champagne

Look for the Gold Seal "Tilt" half gallons—very handsome, very practical.

Bully Hill Winery
Hammondsport, N.Y.
Estab. 1970

If you get to Hammondsport, you must climb Bully Hill and see the Wine Museum and Walter Taylor's small but interesting winery. Just don't tell the people at Taylor's unless you want to involve yourself in internecine warfare. Walter, proprietor of Bully Hill, didn't like the way his family made wine, but evidently the public does. Walter makes his differently. There's room for both.

WHITE

Verdelet Blanc	$3.75	This is from a new hybrid, Seibel 9110. I found the '72 quite good. You're lucky to find it.
Seyval Blanc	$4.00	This is 95% Seyval and 5% Aurora. Clean. Pleasant. Chardonnay-like in taste.
Aurora Blanc	$3.50	100% of Aurora. Light and fruity—Riesling nose.

RED

Chelois Noir	$3.50	I liked the '72. Quite complex mix of Chelois, Cascade, Colobel, and Foch—all hybrid. Bone dry. Ages nicely.

Baco Noir $3.50   A mix of Baco, Cascade,
                                        and Rougons. No water or
                                        sugar added. Will age.

There is a 100% Chancellor Noir, another Seibel hybrid, I
didn't like as well—$4.00. There are also Bully Hill Red, White,
and Pink—very adequate hybrid blends—under $3.00.

Boordy Vineyards
Riderwood, Md. 21139—Penn Yan, N.Y. 14527
Prosser, Wash. 99350
Estab. 1943

The Baltimore Sunpapers are famous. Phil Wagner was the guiding light in making them so. Boordy Wines are famous. Phil
Wagner—ditto

Starting in Riderwood, Maryland, Boordy Wines became such
a success that they have now proliferated to New York and
Washington State. No attempt is made to achieve uniformity.
Each region produces its own variant of well-made inexpensive
wines.

The original Boordy, in the suburbs of Baltimore, established a
reputation far out of proportion to the amount of wine available.
It wasn't fancy. It was what the French call "Pinard"—slang for
a cheap *vin ordinaire*. Well, it couldn't have been that *"ordinaire"* because, first, Seneca foods in Westfield, New York, took
on production of a second Boordy (now at Penn Yan) and more
recently a third is thriving in Washington State, where vinifera
availability, for the first time, provides the novelty.

Most all Boordy wines are vintaged and all indicate the point
of origin on the labels.

Boordy Red	$1.99	75% hybrid and 25% Pinot Noir. Drink fresh or age it a bit. Excellent.
Boordy White	$1.99	90% Seibel hybrid and 10% Semillon.
Boordy Rosé	$1.99	Quite remarkably dry—and with finesse for a pink.
Boordyblumchen	$1.99	In style, a Rhine—in flute bottle. A touch of sweetness.
Pinard (red, white, pink)	$1.69	Unpretentious but remarkably good for such a price.

Konstantin Frank Vinifera Wine Cellars
Hammondsport, N.Y. 14840
Estab. 1961

I realize I have expatiated to quite a degree on Dr. Frank in my remarks on Gold Seal. Suffice it to say, additionally, that he is a peppery little man, a bit of a genius in his way, with an adorable wife who keeps some order in the cellars much as W. C. Fields used to maintain that roll-top desk.

This is a small operation, but oh, my! It has "thrown its beam" far out of proportion to its volume. Dr. Frank has pioneered the making of wines in New York of 100% vinifera varietals—and these of the finest types only. With the exception of Charles Fournier and Widmer to a small degree, he has fought a lonesome fight. The huge companies want no part of the hazards. They are content with their labruscas, hybrids, and the inclusion, in some of their wines, of wine from California. Even Geneva Station considers the vinifera an iffy proposition and opts for the hybrids. Dr. Frank wants no part of them or of labrusca. Taste a Frank Riesling and you're probably drinking the finest wine produced in the Empire State.

QUOTATION: "If these best grape varieties (vinifera) flourish in Chile, and have since 1520, since they were brought there by the monks, then we in Northeast America are now only four hundred and fifty years too late, denying them now"—*Konstantin Frank.*

WHITE

Riesling	$3.00 to $45.00	Seriously, $45 is what Dr. Frank charged for the legendary Riesling Trockenbeerenauslese (like the wine of the Rhineland made from overripe, botrytis-affected grapes, picked one by one). Today, $5 to $6 is more like it. The '68 I tried was round, Riesling-y, great. His wines vary from vintage to vintage, even barrel to barrel.
Gewürztraminer	$5.00 to $6.00	The '68 was a *spätlese* (from selected, late-picked grapes), spicy and just a touch sweet.
Pinot Chardonnay	$6.00 to $8.00	The '69 was superb, the '70 was not as big. True complexity.

There are some red wines—Pinot Noir and Gamay—but the whites are the cream of the crop.

There are a few others: "Five-Two-Seven-Six," which is a white table wine named for its progenitor: Seyve-Villard 5276, an Eastern French hybrid. A little Boordy Cabernet Sauvignon, Pinot Noir, and Semillon Sec will be entering the market from Washington's Yakima—a very little.

O-Neh-Da Vineyard
Conesus, N.Y. 14435
Estab. 1872

Here's another case where the church gets into the wine act. O-Neh-Da. (Oh dear, that name. It means "hemlock," I'm told. Even so, why would Bishop McQuaid want people to drink hemlock?)

At first, only altar wines were made. But after Prohibition the brethren (of the Society of the Divine Word) branched out into regular table wines. Cribari of Fresno, California, now lease and operate the property (primarily to sell altar wines, nationally). That's the same Cribari whose family name appears on some of the Guild labels.

Some Selected Wines are: Haut Sauterne, a Delaware, and a Missouri Riesling (you're right if you're "from Missouri": it's *not* a Riesling). Of late, there are experimental plantings of vinifera (from Gold Seal) and French hybrids.

Widmer's Wine Cellars
Naples, N.Y. 14512
Estab. 1888

This is one of the finest operations in the East (and very lately, in the West as well!).

The first Widmer wine I ever tasted went by the unlikely name of Widmerheimer, and it still does—and it still is a very pleasant white drinkin' wine. But, to my way of thinking, Widmer's best is their Lake Niagara, a "varietal" from this best of labruscas. Niagara is only one of the Lake "varietals" Widmer makes—Elvira, Delaware, Dutchess, Moore's Diamond, Isabella are others. Aren't the words lovely—right out of the Thomas Wolfe school of Americana. You can thank Frank Schoonmaker, as usual, for this distinct advance, for it was he who first suggested the "varietal" group instead of the usual generic blends of New York State Sauterne, New York State Burgundy, etc. None of these generics —vintaged, incidentally—have that unpleasant labrusca smell or flavor. I'm told the main secret is long aging in small cooperage.

Another Widmer first is the outdoor Solera for blending and aging Sherries and Ports, as do the wineries of Jerez in Spain.

Widmer scored another first with its purchase of 500 acres in the Alexander Valley of Sonoma, California, to insure its own supply of California, low-acid wines for mixing and also for bottling as its own thing. Cabernet Sauvignon and Pinot Noir are the first in national distribution and excellent.

The present owner of Widmer is R. T. French Co., well-known for mustard and the annual cookbook awards.

Look for Widmer's New York State Riesling. It's from the Missouri Riesling, a cross of labruscas, though some say there must have been white Riesling somewhere in the family. Sometimes it's even a *spätlese*, ♪when it's *Edelfaule* time in Napoli, New York.♪

Canandaigua Industries
Canandaigua, N.Y.
Estab. 1954

Canandaigua could produce in a half hour what Konstantin Frank makes in a year. In a word, this is a huge operation, some say second only to Taylor-Great Western, some say bigger—and some say third only to Henkel in Germany and Moët in Epernay in production of sparkling wine.

Beginning as bulk producers, they still are, but in the meantime, you know them for the enormously successful Wild Irish Rose—a sweet, pink, labrusca. It came about because "rosé" meant nothing to Americans but "rose" did. On such horseshoe nails are empires lost—or built!

Another name you (or your dad) are likely to know is Virginia Dare. Once a scuppernong-flavored wine of the South, its name had gone west to United Vintners. Canandaigua leased it back and created around it a line of generics composed of California and New York State blends: Burgundy, Sauterne, Rosé, and White as well as Sherries and Ports. No, Virginia, you're not the same girl any more.

Geneva Experiment Station
Geneva, N.Y.

Imagine! From 1933 to 1962 the only grape experimentation permitted in Geneva was to aid and abet the making of grape juice and jelly. That's how strong the W.C.T.U. and the drys per se were in the halls of legislation at Albany. Of course, should a few gallons suddenly start to ferment—well, you couldn't help that.

For the last twelve or thirteen years Geneva has conducted an open operation, in conjunction with Cornell's undergraduate courses in viticulture. The Station is a division of the New York College of Agriculture and Life Sciences at Cornell.

Geneva is devoting its major efforts to "getting closer and closer to vinifera flavor" in labrusca wines—and succeeding. A new grape, Cayuga White, much like a Johannisberg, may become the number one in white-wine making. It is a cross between Seyval, a French hybrid, and Schuyler, a cross between labrusca Ontario and vinifera Zinfandel. It has tested out well and should be sparsely available soon now. Rome—not even Rome, New York—wasn't built in a day!

Chatauqua-Erie
Niagara

The Chatauqua belt along Lake Erie goes back to 1818 when—you guessed it—a Baptist deacon, Elijah Fay, planted some Delaware, Catawba, and Isabella there. Came the *déluge*—Concord. Today the area supplies table grapes, and Concords for Welch's Grape Juice in Brocton, and the "Kosher" Manischewitz in Fredonia and Mogen David of Chicago. "Kosher" in name only—the sweet Concord taste has found a congenial gentile sweet tooth waiting from coast to coast.

Niagara Falls Wine Cellar
Lewiston, N.Y. 14092
Estab. 1972

This new winery occupies the old premises of Chateau Gay, which is today a Canadian operation going by the name of Chateau Gai. This area is opposite the Canadian vineyards, which

are ten times larger in extent. The positioning, almost totally sur-
rounded by water, is perfect for keeping winter temperatures
from dropping too low. Already some vinifera have been planted,
along with the very best varietals, and a splendid sparkling wine,
called Blanc de Blancs and *not* Champagne, is worth seeking out.

THE WINERIES OF
THE HUDSON RIVER REGION

This district, upriver just an hour or two from New York, is reputedly the oldest wine-growing area in the United States. Wine
has been made since those French Protestant refugees I mentioned heretofore started cultivating vinifera (to no avail) back
in 1677.

The first success, and the oldest active winery in the United
States, is the *Brotherhood Wine Co.* in Orange County. Only
fifty miles from the city, people come up to make a day of it, re-
turning with Burgundy or Sauterne by the case, and tired children by the dozen.

The *Hudson Valley Wine Co.,* established 1907 up near High-
land, was formerly known as Bolegnesi. I remember their wines
from early days, right after Prohibition. I think it was their
Delkadét, or some such name as that, that suited me very well.
Now it has been acquired by M. Henri and they in turn by Pep-
siCo, so things should be happening—in a big way.

Benmarl, my favorite, is a little gem of a vineyard-winery up
in Marlboro on the Hudson's left bank. There, charming Mark
Miller, artist turned vintner, has held forth since 1956, though
the vineyard goes back into the distant past. Miller likes to call
Benmarl a "teaching vineyard"—teaching neighboring vintners

how to grow vinifera and what vinifera to grow and—and what French hybrids give the best results in the Hudson Valley.

QUOTATION: "This is more of a crusade than a business"— *Mark Miller.*

One of the inventions of Miller is the Société de Vignerons. Commercial? Sure it is, but fun. You buy "vinerights" in Benmarl. Select two vines from all those growing as "yours" for $100. Pay $30 a year "maintenance" and $15 "dues" and you're entitled to come and pick (if you want to) a case of wine, annually. Over 200 members today account for a fourth of total production.

The Seyval Blanc (1974—$3.25) is exceptional. The Baco Noirs are among the best ('71 and '72). The Johannisberg Riesling '74 was sensational but—alas!—not in *commercial* quantity at the time.

There are two other wineries in the Hudson Valley area: *Royal Wine* and *Mandia.* The latter claims to have been the first to bottle Cold Duck, if that's an honor.

The Wineries and Wines of the Other States

ARIZONA Not much wine activity yet though Arizona produces a large quantity of table and raisin grapes. The Bianes of Brookside have recently established two branches in Arizona and have done a little experimental planting.

ARKANSAS I had a cousin in Little Rock who lost a lot of money in Arkansas yellow diamonds. I don't know if he ever tried his hand at grapes!

When you mention Arkansas wine, eyebrows rise. Well, get 'em right down because Arkansas makes wine, good wine and a lot of it.

The main wine-grape-growing area is in the northwest of the state around Altus and Paris. There's where the *Post Winery* operates under its fourth generation of Posts, since Jacob Post came from Bavaria and settled in Altus in 1872 and set up shop in 1880. Today a family of twelve sturdy Post offspring just about

keep up with a 200-acre vineyard and the 400,000-gallon winery. Campbell's Early is the principal grape—along with Cynthiana and a flock of hybrids. Burgundy, Chianti, Sauterne, and Rhine (about $1.25) and a Brut Champagne (about $5.00) are the principal products, along with Port and Sherry and a strawberry and an apple wine.

Wiederkehr's Wine Cellars, with a storage capacity of over 2 million gallons, is the largest in the South. Established in 1880 by an emigré from Switzerland; bound for Argentina, he got side-tracked in Arkansas, to the benefit of both. Today 1500 cases a day are rolling out to the Arkansas market, with one third going to neighboring states. Burgundy, Chianti, Rhine, Sauterne—plus Cynthiana, Catawba, and Niagara, etc.—plus Champagnes, Cold Duck, and fruit wines make up a comprehensive list. And yes, once in a while a little—a very little—Chardonnay and Johannisberg Riesling find their way into bottles.

Freyaldenhoven's Winery, established 1937, at Morrilton, is under the trade names "Freyaldenhoven" and "Petit Jean"—a family operation.

Cowie's, Henry Sax, and Mount Bethel are other smaller wineries. None of their products leave the state.

FLORIDA   Want any watermelon wine? The state of Florida wants the Weavers, the state's only vintners, to experiment with it. Whether they will, deponent sayeth not. But meantime *Bartel's Winery* at Pensacola is doing all right, making wine from such plebeian sources as muscadine and scuppernong grapes—and yes, blackberries. The 50,000 bottles they produce in a winery under their restaurant don't get very far afield so you'll have to go to Florida to try it. Be sure you ask for Lake Emerald, from a new wine grape Ralph Weaver and his son have developed by crossing a vinifera and a local muscadine.

GEORGIA As you'd expect, peaches get into the act down Georgia way. The *Monarch Wine Co.* makes more peach wine, they claim, than anyone else in the world! Gee!

IDAHO I'm afraid even the friendliest local wine dealer won't be able to supply a bottle of Chelois from Idaho Wine and Grape Grower's *Troy Winery*. The University of Idaho is gung ho for a wine industry in the state and is working through R. Bruce Higgins, a research co-ordinator at the U. of I. and a partner of the winery. Vinifera are coming next, we're told. We shall see.

ILLINOIS For Illinois, read *"Mogen David, Chicago"*—producing kosher wine from grapes brought in from hither and yon.

INDIANA I don't know what future there is for commercial vintners in Indiana because I remember, when a guest lecturer at the University of Indiana, at Bloomington, that it seemed every man, woman, and . . . young adult was making his own wine in the cellar. I also remember the president of the university having to take me off campus to offer me a glass of Sherry. (It wasn't two years later that I read of a class in "Wine Appreciation" being offered at the University of Indiana! The more things change, the more they're *not* the same.)

Grapes for wine are not a new crop to Indiana. In the 1850s winegrowing was a respectable industry. But it took the Indiana legislature's 1971 "limited wineries" measure to start things humming again.

Carl Banholzer (formerly of Tabor Hill in Michigan) has 44 acres under vine and 200 in his mind. Primarily they will be the French hybrids. The first crush was in '75.

Indiana's first "going concern" is the *Treaty Line Wine Cellar* near Connersville in southern Indiana. Donald McDaniel is the entrepreneur. He has already made a little red and white table wine—plans more from all the hybrids and some vinifera. Near Bloomington, Professor William Oliver has a small hybrids vineyard. Among other things, it supplied the grapes for Treaty Line's first crush.

LOUISIANA, goodness knows, should have wine to go with all that good food but not much has been done yet. Wonder if that grand old man of things gastronomic in New Orleans, Lysle Aschaffenberger of the Pontchartrain Hotel, would like a nice scuppernong to go with his jambalaya?

MARYLAND Maryland's two claims to fame (in wine, that is) are a century and a half apart: Major John Adlum, who found the Catawba growing in Maryland in 1802 and gave it its name, and Philip Wagner, whom I discussed in my comments on *Boordy*, the vineyards he first invented at Riderwood, Maryland (and later expanded to Westfield, New York, and Prosser, Washington). Other wineries: *Caroli, Montbray* (which is marketing a little vinifera—Maryland's first since Lord Baltimore made an effort in 1662).

MICHIGAN The Lake State, fourth nationally in wine, has two feathers in its cap in the wine world—one noble and one dubious.

The salutary one is that Michigan is the birthplace and home of the American Wine Society; the other, Cold Duck was born here!

The American Wine Society was founded in 1967 to "further the knowledge, appreciation and enjoyment of fine American wines." It is an eleemosynary organization of professional wine makers, home wine makers, and just plain devotees of wine and those who want to be. Ten dollars sent to charming Margaret Jackisch, Executive Secretary, 4218 Rosewold Ave., Royal Oak, Mich. 48073, will make you one of the anointed.

Cold Duck, the name that wagged the wine, was originally a mix of New York Champagne and California Sparkling Burgundy. The name derived from a pun on the German words "Kalte *Ende*" (cold end), a name applied to the frugal German habit of mixing all the wines from various partly empty bottles at the end of a party, and "Kalte *Ente*" (cold duck). It can be made of well-nigh anything that sparkles and is pinkish red. I shall never forget the shock I had when first seeing "Cold Duck" emblazoned on a pile of cases waiting for shipment in *Bordeaux!* So help me. The "Duck" is today flying on only one wing, so the trade tells me.

Michigan Wineries, with its *Warner Vineyards* division, is the largest in Michigan. It makes everything from still and sparkling grape juice to concentrates, Champagnes, and berry wines. Their Vineyard Red, White, and Rosé are well worth trying.

Bronte, one of the oldest (1933), was the first to make a Champagne in Michigan and one of the first to fling tradition, and Concord grapes, to the wind, and produce wines from hybrids and labruscas other than Concord. Sister Lakes White is worth a go.

St. Julian and *Vendramino* are other Michigan wineries of consequence.

In the mid-'60s a Big Ten football player and steel salesman decided neither pigskin nor girders were for him, and Leonard Olson and his lovely Ellen bought *Tabor Hill* in Berrien County near Buchanan. His modest plan was to make not the most, just the *best,* wines in Michigan! Tomorrow, the world. Growing only vinifera and French hybrids, Tabor is turning out over 13,000 cases and expects to double that by 1977. I found the Vidal Blanc and Baco Noir excellent ($3.50) and the very limited Riesling and Chardonnay ($7.00) remarkable. Cuvée Blanc, a blend, is a find at $2.89. With help and advice from experts of Geisenheim, the great German enological school, maybe Olson will achieve his goal sooner than you'd think.

Most Michigan wines are sold at the wineries. A few are achieving state-wide and out-of-state distribution (Tabor and Warner are two). And, of course, you can always get them at the White House—depending upon who is President, of course.

MISSISSIPPI has no commercial winery, though it is now also theoretically wet. The state is working on the subject.

MISSOURI   In 1866, Missouri became number two in wine-growing, supplanting Ohio, the previous number two. A century later things vinous are on the move again. If you're from Missouri and have to be shown, there are eight bonded wineries now operating, five of them opened quite recently.

Bardenheier Wine Cellars of St. Louis, established in 1874, is by far the largest. For a long time they blended and bottled California wines for the Middle West. Now they are growing some of their own grapes and making their own Missouri wines—mostly of Catawba and French hybrids.

The German influx led to Missouri's wine heyday. In 1847 *Stone Hill Winery* was set up and by 1870 was said to be second largest in the United States. The grape used was the Virginia Seedling. I never heard of it either! The wines bore such catchy names as Hermannsberger and Starkenberger. Today Stone Hill makes nine wines, including Missouri Riesling, Catawba, Niagara, and Cynthiana.

There is a cluster of vineyards around St. James: *Stolz, St. James*, and *Roseti. Mount Pleasant* is a small winery, established in 1881, and rediscovered and rededicated by the Dressels in 1968.

The most exciting development in Missouri is the new research and development project, known as the Grape Research Demonstration Project, of the University of Missouri. Experimental vineyards are being set up and planted with a great many varieties—from vinifera to hybrids to labrusca.

NEW ENGLAND Despite my personal devotion to the area—thanks to college in Hanover, courting at Wellesley, lecturing at the Arnold Arboretum, lobstering in Maine, skiing in Vermont, antiquing in Rhode Island, theatergoing in Connecticut—I would not honestly call New England a wine threat!

Grapes were once grown in Martha's Vineyard and Nantucket and wine was made; Connecticut has grapevines in its state seal and has a few tiny vineyards; Vermont has reduced its license fees and Maine is "studying things." Only New Hampshire has done anything in a biggish way. In Laconia, hard by Lake Winnipesaukee, a family named Canepa founded the *White Mountain Vineyards*. Now, many farmers in the area are raising grapes for the Canepas.

NEW JERSEY In my opinion, New Jersey's claim to fame lies with the apple more than the grape. My friends at *Laird & Co.* (since 1780—they say the country's oldest distillery) make the best apple brandy outside of Normandy, and some apple wine as well. (If you've never tasted Farmer's Bishop, you should: heat Laird or Hildick applejack, add hot cider and baked oranges stuck with cloves. It's the regular Christmas drink at our house.)

Renault near Egg Harbor is probably the largest in the state. Renault Champagne combines California and labrusca wines—one of the first to blend East and West. *Gross, Tomasello, Egg Harbor Winery* are others.

But probably the worst handicap to New Jersey wine is the fact that Thomas Welch came to Vineland and started his grape juice empire there—in that bone-dry community. Serves him right—a century later, long after his death, the company discovered yeast and fermentation!

NORTH CAROLINA was the pre-eminent scuppernong state. The University of North Carolina is working wholeheartedly to make it the muscadine state once again. (It *is* a bit more poetic than Tarheel.) De-emphasizing muscadine, a certain H. Bryan Doble of Tryon is busily proving that viniferas can be happy in North Carolina. In seven years he hasn't lost a vine.

OHIO   When you mention the wines of Ohio, once the number one wine state in the Union, you mention Nicholas Longworth at the same time, for Longworth (great-grandfather of Speaker Longworth of the House) is as intimately associated with the wine of Ohio as Dom Perignon was with the Champagnes of France. In 1823 he planted the first vineyards along the banks of the Ohio River at Cincinnati, which launched a thousand casks! He made White Catawba wine and the first American sparkling wine which he called Sparkling Catawba. No essay on United States wine in general or Ohio wine in particular is ever complete without reference to the immortal lines limned to the glory of Catawba by none other than H. W. Longfellow:

> Very good in its way is the Verzenay,
>   Or the Sillery, soft and creamy;
> But Catawba wine has a taste more divine,
>   More dulcet, delicious and dreamy.

Ohio's wines were, and are, made in two basic areas—south, along the Ohio, and north, near Cleveland and Sandusky on Lake Erie. The Ohio wine industry suffered two devastating blows: (1) the so-called "vine sickness" or plague which decimated the vineyards of Longworth and others; and (2) Prohibition. Of course the latter hit other states as well, but few had as much to lose as Ohio.

Today, west of Cleveland are two sizable wineries: *Avon Lake* and *Dover;* and east, two others: *Steuk's* and *Mantey's*. But the most fascinating part of the Ohio wine story are the vineyards on the little islands offshore in Lake Erie. *Meier's*, of Sandusky and Cleveland, and Ohio's leading vintners, own and work some of these island vineyards. *Lonz* and *Heineman* are small makers there. Meier's wines are to be found beyond the confines of O-hi-o and I suggest you search out their Champagnes, still wines, and Sherry, made by Henry O. Sonneman's Meier's Wine Cellars—among the very best in the East. His son and daughter, Jack and Janet, have a young winery too called *Château Jac Jan* —get it?

OREGON   The new "gold rush" is the wine rush to Oregon and Washington. To enologists who believe that good wine grapes require cool weather, slow ripening, harsh soil conditions that make a vine work hard, Oregon is the *cave* of the future.

Oregon's story, which began in the 1800s, ground to a halt at Prohibition time and wasn't updated until 1963. It was then that a Dick Sommer bonded a winery in the Umpqua Valley. In 1966 a certain David Lett started the *Eyrie Vineyard* in Dundee. In 1967 the *Charles Coury* label was first seen. Dick Erath planted the *Erath Vineyards* in 1968, and *Oak Knoll* came along in 1971. *Hillcrest* is another top-drawer winery and top medal winner. All of these men feel Oregon's the place for *distinctive*— fruity, zesty, crisp—wines, with more zip and get-up-'n'-go than California. Coury's Riesling ($2.85) and Eyrie's ($4.50) are outstanding. Oregon seems to be "right" for Riesling—and for Pinot Noir. At the State Fair in Salem, Oregon (1974), Coury's and Erath's Pinot Noir took first and second respectively; in Chardonnay, Coury took first; in Riesling, Hillcrest was first, Coury second, and Erath third.

You'll have to go to Oregon to try most of these.

PENNSYLVANIA   Pennsylvania is no newcomer to grape growing. Today, Pennsylvania is fifth in grapes—but most of these are Concords and find their lackluster way into grape juice bottles. As long ago as William Penn's time, in the late seventeenth century, the vine was planted but, being vinifera, as usual failed.

At the time of the Revolution a man named John Alexander discovered native wild grapes growing near Philadelphia, domesticated some, and gave his name, Alexander, to one of the country's most famous wine grapes.

A bit later the vine moved west—to the Pittsburgh area—and to the shores of Lake Erie, not far from New York's Chatauqua belt.

The problem in Pennsylvania was that a commercial vintner had to sell his wares entirely through the Pennsylvania State Store system—a severe limitation which, in 1967, was finally rescinded. Now wineries can sell up to 100,000 gallons a year where they will.

Almost immediately *Presque Isle Winery* near North East set up shop and produced viniferas and hybrids of quality. And in 1969 the *Penn-Shore Vineyards* followed, making estate-bottled table wines and the first Pennsylvania Champagne.

And even more recently—May of 1974 to be exact—*Bucks Country Vineyards* opened their doors in Bucks County near New Hope to much fanfare. Some of the hybrid wines were even selected by the glamorous Heublein for inclusion in their "Wine Discoveries of the World" tastings in Vegas, Chicago, and New York. Sandy McNally, Heublein's vaunted wine scout, selected Chelois, Baco Noir, Catawba, and Delaware.

SOUTH CAROLINA is another state where, in theory though not in practice, the Shirley Temple is the strongest drink allowed. However, there is an absentee-landlorded winery in Chesterfield County—big, too—making wine for the Canandaigua people in New York.

TENNESSEE There isn't any commercial winery as such in Tennessee but I include it because there are true wine lovers and highly knowledgeable wine amateurs. My good friend Homer Blitch (sic) of Nashville tells me that *his* good friend

144

S. McPheeters Glasgow (sic) has a farm in Cookeville growing French-American hybrids and has produced some "excellent, commercial-grade white wine," but very little. He also introduced me to the Champagne made by Judge William Beach of Clarksville when he isn't "judging" at the Montgomery County criminal court—first rate, too. A Tennessee Viticultural and Enological Society has been formed to further a wine industry in the state, and the University of Tennessee is studying possibilities.

In discussing wine in the Southeast there are several things to consider. There is a strong vein of Bible Belt-ism running throughout, evidenced by dry counties, many teetotaling people, and a general anti-alcohol climate—this despite the many references (and salutary ones) to wine throughout the Good Book. A puzzlement. And this is the area where the scuppernong, beloved of Thomas Wofe, long held sway. This is a member of the *Vitis rotundifolia* family or, easier to say, a muscadine.

UTAH, NEW MEXICO—not much wine news to report. Ditto for other states not mentioned. Please, no brickbats if I'm wrong.

VIRGINIA, once the leader in attempting to make wine from European vinifera vines, is today best known for the wine Virginia Dare. The name had passed on to Guild in California but, by franchise, a Virginia Dare with the original scuppernong flavor is made by *Richard's Wine Cellar,* largest in the state. *Woburn, Laird, Dixie, Southland,* and *Grey* are other Virginia wineries—for the most part selling locally.

Stop press! A newcomer has newly come. The Zonin Wine Co. (headquarters—Europe) has started planting and planning for 1979 or 1980 production of the best vinifera varietals. Two other vinifera vineyards—1975 arrivals—are Farselu and Meredyth. Things are looking up in the Old Dominion.

WASHINGTON is the third state in grape production and seventh in wine. The Yakima Valley is regarded by many as the peer of, if not greater than, Napa. When such a judge of wine as the late Charles van Kriedt (he of the California "Wineletter") stated—referring to a Ste. Michelle White Riesling '72, "One of the best Johannisbergers we have ever tasted ($3.95), and the Chenin Blanc '72 was utterly delicious ($3.95)," they must be doing something very right at *American Wine Growers.*

In the fall of 1974, in Los Angeles, the same Johannisberg Riesling was picked number one, from among fourteen American and four German Rieslings. American is a combine of six or eight wineries, largest now in the state. Ste. Michelle is their name for vinifera varietals, which are slowly achieving national distribution.

Santa Rosa, Alhambra, and *Werberger* are other Washington wineries of note. Washington grows all three grape types successfully—vinifera, labrusca, and hybrids—but the story, circa 1974, is in these figures: acreage—Concord, 18,600; hybrid 1500; vinifera 2300. However, vinifera has increased, since 1968, fivefold; hybrids, threefold; and Concord only twice.

WISCONSIN Not really a wine state. Cows don't mind but grapes object to so few days between killing frosts of spring and fall. The Wallersheim family in Sauk Prairie has restored an old winery on the Wisconsin River and re-established a vineyard. To date they have specialized in cherry wine but they promise estate-bottled grape wines shortly. Dairymen—cheese it!

MISCELLANEOUS

IOWA, OKLAHOMA, NEBRASKA This is 2-4D country. This weed killer, used for corn, can't distinguish vines from weeds! Hence, no vines survive! Pity.

The Wines of the Other Americas

ARGENTINA

The Argentine is the most important wine-producing country in the Western world. There—I've said it!

Producing about twice as much wine as the United States (about 550 million gallons a year), Argentina ranks fourth in volume among the nations of the world (unless the U.S.S.R. wants to make something of it) but her own 26 million people drink 90% of it. That's to the tune of 29 gallons per person, while we have yet to reach 2! Only France, Italy, and Spain exceed her production or consumption. However, the vast majority of the wines are from the Criolla grape, a close relative of our Mission. It makes a harsh, tannic wine which, when I was there, sold for about thirty-five cents a liter. The vinifera production is still limited but growing in quantity and improving in quality at

a rapid rate. Keep your eyes open for the wines of Argentina—they're coming bung ho, our way.

Seventy per cent of Argentina's wine comes from the province of Mendoza in the far west of the country, hard by the heroic Andes. The province of San Juan to the north produces 20% and Rio Negro to the south (to which many vintners look for the greatest future in winegrowing) yields 6% today.

Mendoza is—or rather was—a desert, until someone suggested harnessing the melting snows from the mountains and sluicing them through irrigation ditches to the thirsty vines. Result—absolutely incredible yields of fruit from varieties of every type. And to handle the colossal yield, the Argentines have constructed gigantic wineries, modern and shiny, with every type of modern wine-making equipment, as well as a superb government control agency. Bodegas Peñaflor is second in size only to Gallo, and possibly United Vintners or Taylor, in the hemisphere. Giol, government-owned, is nearly as large. With most wines reaching our shores with a $3.00 ticket or less, Argentina is a good place to look for decent wines at a decent price.

The export wines of the Argentine are made from the premium vinifera types of Europe: Cabernet Sauvignon, Riesling, Pinot Blanc, Pinot Gris, Malbeck (with a *k*), Merlot, and the like. I think it can be unequivocally stated that the reds are (or were) superior to the whites. This need not always be. Argentines are learning to drink (and ship) white wines fresh and young, and not four and five years old, yellow and somewhat over the top. Then the whites will be uniformly as good as ones I tasted at Norton, Suter, Orfila, and Bianchi.

Argentine wines to look for: A new label, "Andean Vineyards," is very much to the fore. Born to the energetic Byron Tosi, its vice-chairman, as wet nurse, a number of wineries are collaborating under this label to offer a very good Cabernet Sauvignon (from Bodega Orfila) at about $3.35, a ditto Riesling (Peñaflor), a Pinot Blanc (also Peñaflor), and a Pinot Gris Rosé (Bodega

Santa Ana)—all at about $2.90. They also handle distribution for Calero, another Rosé in an odd liter bottle shaped like a *bota* or wineskin.

Another label you'll see is that of Trumpeter. These wines are the unlikely offspring of Scottish and Newcastle, the British brewers and pub operators. Two excellent Trumpeters are the Cabernet Sauvignon (100% varietal) and Cabernet Malbeck (a blend)—both backed by considerable promotion and gaining distribution.

The more traditional family Argentine wines may need a bit of searching out. Worth the effort are the wines of Lopez, especially Rincon and Château Vieux.

Suter and Bianchi (Seagram imports through Browne Vintners) produce some excellent wines. I particularly enjoyed Suter's Pinot Blanco and Bianchi's Dona Valentin and Valentin La Corrado (which won a medal in Budapest)—also Chablis and Rosé.

Bodegas Arizu is one of Argentina's largest and best producers —look for their Valroy, a rather complex red; Cuesta del Parral, a Merlot varietal; and a very decent "Champagne." Their Cava Privada wines—limited quantity—probably are not available yet but they show what five to ten years in the bottle can do for Cabernet, Malbeck and Merlot blends. Norton, another fine bodega, has Boston and Los Angeles distribution—maybe more by now. Their Malbeck and Sauvignon are very good.

Sparkling wines also come in for attention. M. Chandon is one company, affiliated with you-know-whom. Crillon and Monitor are brands produced by the Crillon Winery, a Seagram operation.

B R A Z I L

You are not likely to encounter many Brazilian bottles in the United States, though quite a bit of Brazilian wine is made for

home consumption. After all, sometimes we forget that Brazil was colonized by the Portuguese—no mean wine drinkers, they!

Brazil sits astride the equator, not exactly a location conducive to the exploitation of the vine. As you would expect, the prime winegrowing area is the state of Rio Grande do Sul, about as far south (and hence about as cool) as you can get in Brazil without finding yourself in Uruguay or Argentina. I was surprised to find the United States labruscas and hybrids leading the list of grape varieties: Isabella is the leader, but there are also Dutchess, Niagara and—yes—Concord. Barbera, Cabernet, Riesling, Trebbiano are grown for the better wines. The biggest producer goes by the catchy name of "Indústria, Comércio e Navegação, Sociedade Vinícola Rio Grandense, Ltda." Their monopole is Granja União. Other important names are Michielon, Dreher, Antunes.

No one can currently say that the wines of Brazil are anything to write home to Napa or Naples about. But perhaps there is a light, or a "white," at the end of the tunnel. It has been announced that National Distillers has bought an interest in Vinhos Finos Santa Rosa and has shipped them 70,000 of Almadén's cuttings of the best varietals for planting. By 1981 we should know.

CANADA

I'm glad not to be writing this piece a few years ago when I first tasted Canadian wine. It wouldn't have been a very laudatory critique, as I found the wines I tasted pretty awful. But then, in 1975 I attended a tasting of some of the current wines and found a vast improvement.

In 1916 most of Canada opted for Prohibition. In 1927 they opted back again. This, coupled with the usual unsophisticated taste of a basically Anglo-Saxon country for sweet glop, threw up a pretty good road block against decent table wines. The sweet, dessert, fortified "Ports" were the order of the day until quite recently. In 1969 consumption was 9.5 million gallons of wine of 14% to 20% alcohol, compared to 4.8 million gallons of table wine below 14%. By 1973 the figures had reversed: 14 million gallons of table wine compared to 11 million gallons of dessert—25 million gallons in all, plus 10 million of imported wines. Per capita consumption had climbed from half a gallon in 1964 to 1.1 gallons a decade later.

Everybody knows the apocryphal tale of Leif the Lucky, reputedly the first European to see the shores of the North American continent. So covered were they with wild grapes that he dubbed Newfoundland, Vineland. Although there are fragmentary accounts of wine making before, it is generally agreed that John Schiller, a German, was the first to set up a true winery. That was 1811. By the turn of the century Ontario had a thriving wine industry in the Niagara peninsula which sticks down into the United States across from Buffalo, between Lakes Erie and Ontario. Three quarters of Canadian wine is produced there, the remainder in the Far West in the Okanagan Valley of British Columbia.

Bright's of Toronto and Niagara Falls is Canada's largest, and possibly best, winery. Bright's makes wine from labrusca, hybrids, and even from vinifera. I found their Chardonnay and Champagne (100% Chardonnay incidentally) truly excellent but, as yet, experimental. A certain Monsieur de Chaunac deserves the credit—and got it by having a French hybrid, Seibel 9549, named De Chaunac. In a true ecumenical gesture, Bright's competitors, Château-Gai, also in the Niagara area, use the grape to make one of their best wines. Their Maréchal Foch and Gamay Beaujolais I rated 16 out of 20—first rate. There is now also a Château-Gay across in New York, at Lewiston. Château-Gai is probably Canada's best-known wine name, shipping to the United States and even to Great Britain. Jordan, Andrés, and Château Cartie are other well-known names in Canada, the latter owned by the famous Labatt ale people.

Way off in British Columbia, across from Washington, many of the wines are made from varying percentages of California-grown grapes. Another Hungarian—they do crop up—named Eugene Rittich felt the Okanagan Valley, because of the temperature-moderating lakes, could grow grapes. He was correct and now a quota demanding 65% or more of British Columbian grapes can be sensibly applied and enforced. Calona, Gintner, Beau Séjour, and Andrés are well-known names here though you'll probably have to go up there to taste them. A few other wineries are located hither and yon, in other provinces, primarily in the East. By the way, Canadian labels don't state vintage or alcoholic content.

CHILE

The first South American wine I ever tasted was an Undurraga Riesling. I found it good. I still do.

There is not much doubt that the wines of Chile are the best (with perhaps a desultory argument from some specific Argentine wine) on the continent, and have been since 1851 when Silvestre Ochagavia, the Chilean Harászthy, began importing

French vines and French vintners, mostly from the Bordeaux area. Today, the wines and methods have a distinctly Bordelaise flavor.

As every school child knows, Chile is very long and very thin. Grapes are grown from top to bottom but the best wines come from the central portion, around the city of Santiago and between the river valleys of the Maipo and Aconcagua. North of that is Muscat table-grape land, while south is País country—the País being Chile's Criolla or *vin ordinaire* grape. But in between are produced remarkably good wines from Cabernet Sauvignon, Merlot, Malbeck, Semillon, Sauvignon, Pinot Blanc, Pinot Gris, and Riesling—to name some.

Almost all Chilean vineyards are irrigated, just as in Argentina, and the yield is correspondingly enormous. Imagine a Napa farmer being told to expect 12 tons and more per acre of Cabernet Sauvignon! Interestingly, the grapelands of Chile have not expanded since 1938—this by law. It was Chile's way of attacking an alcoholism problem, or so they thought. It worked, too. Today, a Chilean drinks 11 gallons per annum; in the 1930s he consumed over 15.

Another development is the signing of an agreement by most of the major producers to give Seagram (Browne Vintners) the sole marketing rights for Chilean wines in the States and Canada —under their own labels and also under the Bon Sol umbrella brand of Browne Vintners.

Some of the Chilean wines I have enjoyed have been the aforementioned Undurraga in their familiar bocksbeutel flask, modeled after the German Steinwein bottle. The Cabernet Sauvignon, Rhine, and Pinot Noir are especially recommended— and weigh in under $3.00 except for the "Cab" at about $3.40.

Concha y Toro is another favorite of mine. I have yet to have a poor bottle. The Cabernet Sauvignon is outstanding, as are the Rosé and the Riesling—and, if you're lucky enough to find it, Casillero del Diablo.

Other companies and brands worth looking for are Santa Rita Burgundy, Gran Vino Tinto and Gran Vino para Banquetes; Canepa's Chilean Cabernet; San Pedro's Gato Negro with a black cat on the label (black cats certainly do get around); and Tocornal Chilean Riesling. Cousiño Macul is another good name. Most of these wines come in the flask-type bottle.

MEXICO

I remember, the first thing I saw on my last visit to Mexico City was a full-page newspaper ad by the House of Pedro Domecq, apologizing to the people of Mexico for its inability to keep the supply of Domecq wines equal to the demand. I thought to myself, Here's a presumption—that is, until I tasted Domecq's Los Reyes red against other Mexican wines. Then I could understand the ad, as well as the need for it! Los Reyes is a new dimension in Mexican viticulture.

Imported wines (which means ours too, you know) are prohibitively expensive because of import duties. I presume we retal-

iate, as I see very few Mexican wines on our shelves, even in California, so that an exhaustive dissertation on Mexican wine is hardly of much moment here.

The making of wine is very ancient in Mexico, going back to Cortez in the early sixteenth century. Cortez made it obligatory for land grantees to plant the grape. So successful were the new vintners that Spanish wine makers began to feel the pinch and had King Philip forbid new planting and order the uprooting of existing vineyards. Padre Miguel Hidalgo, leader of the anti-Spanish revolution, in 1810, started things going again and Porfirio Diaz, in 1876, with the help of one of the California Concannons, replanted with better vinifera stock from California.

The Madero revolution of 1910 nearly finished the wine industry of Mexico. If it hadn't been for one man, Nazario Garza, there probably would be only pulque, tequila, and Coke to drink in Mexico. Garza was a politician and a visionary. With the help of Davis-trained sons and some fortuitous political appointments, he was able to acquire and plant hundreds of acres to the grape. His is today Mexico's largest wine enterprise. He even uses the famous name of Paternina of Spain, under a license arrangement, on some of the better wines.

PERU

I'll have to pass this one too. Wine *is* made—not too much—around Lima and Cuzco. Pisco brandy is more their thing, distilled from the Muscat.

URUGUAY

Uruguayans will have to forgive me but I know little about their wines. I know that, for so small a country, they produce and drink a whale of a lot of wine.

REPRISE

I have said before that, insofar as wine in the Americas is concerned, I am, to quote Mary Martin (quoting Oscar Hammerstein), "a cockeyed optimist."

As I write this, there is a glut of wine the world over—in California as well as in most of Europe. I recognize all too well the enormous amount of work and money involved in making wine, and the inexorable laws of supply and demand that may make these expenditures less than fruitful for a period. Greatly increased plantings, together with lack of storage facilities—cooperage, tanks, etc.—for 4-million-ton crops (California alone) may paint a pretty bleak picture. But if you weigh this against the normal population increase, the new interest of the younger people in this drink of moderation, the improvements in quality devolving from better grapes and larger percentiles of superior varieties in the blends, and the more sensible prices of the best varietal labels, I am more than sanguine, I am enthusiastic for the long term.

"Santé," Wines of All the Americas.

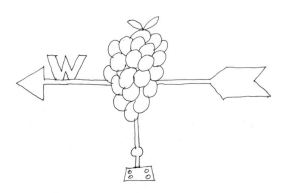

Index

Italy, 9, 24
Ives grape, 29

Jackisch, Margaret, 138
Jesuit Fathers, 88
Johannisberg Riesling (*see* specific wineries); grape, 31
Jordan wines, 152

Kentucky, 116
Korbel, 65–67
Kornell, Hanns, 59
Kornell, Hanns, Cellars, 59–60
Krug, Charles, Winery, 44–46

Labatt, 152
Labeling, 15, 21–22ff.
Labrusca grapes, 4, 5, 19, 28–29. *See also* specific grapes, wineries
Labrusca Red, 124
Laird & Co., 141
Laird wines, 145
Lake Country (wine), 121
Lake Emerald, 136
Lake Niagara, 130
Lamont, M., 111
Latour, Georges, 40
Leif the Lucky, 116–17, 151
Lejon, 72ff.
Lett, David, 143
Llords & Elwood, 91–93
Longworth, Nicholas, 142
Lonz wines, 142–43
Lopez wines, 149
Los Reyes, 154
Louisiana, 138
Luper, Jerry, 56

McCrea, Fred, 64
McDaniel, Donald, 137
McNally, Sandy, 144
Maine, 13, 141
Malbeck, 148ff.
Malvasia, 44, 88, 105, 110
Mandia, 134
Mantey's, 142
Maréchal Foch, 152; grape, 29
Martini, Louis M., 32, 54

Martini, Louis Peter, 54
Martini and Sterling, 30
Martini (Louis M.) Winery, 54–56
Maryland, 138
Masson, Paul, 28, 79–82, 115
Mayacamas, 47–49
Meier's, 142
Mendocino, 108
Meredyth wines, 145
Merlot, 47, 55, 148, 153; grape, 30
Metric system, 13
Mexico, 6, 154–55
Meyer, Otto, 79
Michigan, 138–40
Michigan Wineries, 139
Michelon wines, 150
Miller, Mark, 4, 133–34
Mini-climates, 15
Mirassou Vineyards, 82–84
Misch, R. J., 103
Mission Fathers, 18
Mississippi, 140
Missouri, 140
Missouri Riesling, 129
Mogen David, 132, 137
Monarch Wine Co., 137
Mondavi, Peter, 44
Mondavi, Robert, 44, 51–52
Mondavi Vineyards (brand), 46
Mondavi (Robert) Winery, 51–54
Monitor wines, 149
Montbray wines, 138
Monterey Riesling, 83
Monterey Vineyards, 102–3
Montrachet, 115
Moore's Diamond grape, 29
Morrow brandy, 113
Moscato Canelli, 110
Moselle, 96
Mountain Folle Blanche, 54
Mount Bethel, 136
Mount Pleasant, 140
Mouvedre, 106
Muscadelle de Bordelaise, 60

Date Due

Library Bureau Cat. No. 1137